PSYCHOLOGICAL TRAUMA:
Healing Its Roots in Brain, Body, and Memory

Dawson Church, PhD

Published by Energy Psychology Press
3340 Fulton Rd., #442, Fulton, CA 95439
www.energypsychologypress.com

ISBN# 978-1-60415-261-6

This publication demonstrates an impressive personal improvement tool. It is not a substitute for training in psychology or psychotherapy. Nothing contained herein is meant to replace qualified medical advice. The author urges the reader to use these techniques under the supervision of a qualified therapist or physician. The author and publisher do not assume responsibility for how the reader chooses to apply the techniques herein.

This monograph and other Energy Psychology Press publications use the APA's style guidelines (American Psychological Association, 2009). Many scientific studies are cited, and the references are listed at the end of the book. Often, the percentage of change in a symptom is listed, as in "pain dropped by an average of 68%." Every percentage quoted in this manual is "statistically significant" at the level of $p < .05$ or better, unless otherwise noted. We do not, however, quote the degree of statistical significance in the text. The reason for this omission is that this monograph is intended for the use of lay readers, rather than being a professional textbook. So while it is based on the scientific literature, technical details such as p values are omitted.

Second Edition

Contents

About Dawson Church

Dawson Church, PhD is the author the award-winning and best-selling book *The Genie in Your Genes: Epigenetic Medicine and the New Biology of Intention.* He is a graduate of Baylor University (Mass Media) and Holos University (Integrative Healthcare) and is certified in Energy Psychology (CEHP #2016). He is the editor of the peer-reviewed journal *Energy Psychology,* and has published many scientific research studies on problems such as PTSD, anxiety, and depression (www.EnergyPsychologyJournal.org). He founded the non-profit Veterans Stress Project to provide free PTSD counseling to returning war veterans (www.StressProject.org). He provides consulting services to organizations and teams, showing how to utilize energy psychology to increase productivity and reduce stress in time frames that are much briefer than those found in conventional therapies. He manages EFT Universe, one of the largest alternative medicine sites on the Internet (www.EFTuniverse.com). You can download his free *EFT Mini-Manual* at www.DawsonGift.com.

Psychological Trauma

Pervasive Psychological Trauma

Psychological trauma is widespread. While news reports focus on the high levels of PTSD found in veterans, trauma is far more prevalent in the civilian population than most people realize. Since the wars in Iraq and Afghanistan began in 2001, far more Americans have died at the hands of family members than have been killed in the Middle East. Women are twice as likely to be victims of domestic violence than they are to get breast cancer (van der Kolk, 2014, p. 348).

Much of this violence affects children. According to a report by the U.S. Department of Health and Human Services, 60% of older children had witnessed or experienced victimization in the past year. Close to half had experienced physical assault, and 25% had witnessed domestic or community violence (U.S. Department of Health and Human Services, 2012). Twice as many children are killed by firearms as by cancer.

Incest, the sexual abuse of a child by a family member, was once thought to be uncommon. In 1975, an authoritative source, the *Comprehensive Textbook of Psychiatry*, concluded that, "incest is extremely rare, and does not occur in more than 1 out of 1.1 million people" (Freedman, Kaplan & Sadock, 1975). However, recent estimates are that one in 10 boys has been molested, and one in five girls, usually by a family member (Gorey & Leslie, 1997).

Clearly, an experience of this physical and psychological magnitude could have a traumatic impact. But what's the dividing line between a bad experience and a traumatic one? In Clinical EFT workshops (Emotional Freedom Techniques), we use these four criteria to identify a traumatic event. It must:

- Be a perceived threat to the person's physical survival.
- Overwhelm their coping capacity, producing a sense of powerlessness.
- Produce a feeling of isolation, aloneness.

- Violate their expectations.

It's clear that a serious auto accident, a rape, or a physical assault might meet the criteria for a traumatic event. Yet many childhood events that are barely remembered might also have contributed to traumatization. Take the story told by Martie, a 45-year-old psychotherapist attending an EFT workshop:

> When I was growing up, I idolized my older brother Gary. But he was pretty rough with me. He was 6 years older than I was. One day when I was 3 and he was 9, he wanted to have a "wrestling match." He "won" by lying on top of me. I couldn't breathe, and I began to panic. Gary just laughed when he saw me struggling. I almost passed out. When he rolled off of me, I began to cry uncontrollably. My mother came in, and I tried to explain what happened. He told her it was nothing; I was just being a crybaby. Mom told me, "Big girls don't cry."

This experience meets all four criteria for a traumatizing event. When Gary lay on top of her, 3-year-old Martie felt as though she was going to die. It was *a perceived threat to her physical survival.* She tried to cope by pushing him off, but because he was so much larger, she was unable to. *Her attempt to cope was futile, and she felt powerless.* Being almost smothered by her brother *violated her expectation* that other members of the family would keep her safe. Her brother calling her a crybaby, and her mother supporting him by telling Martie that "Big girls don't cry" produced *a feeling of isolation, that she was all alone* in dealing with her fear.

Most people had several childhood experiences that met these criteria. Some of us had many. Participants in EFT workshops frequently work on healing the emotional impact of these events. EFT is a simple method that combines acupressure with elements of cognitive and exposure therapies. Cognitive therapies address how we see the world through thoughts or "cognitions" that also shape our behavior. Exposure therapies focus on the therapeutic value of remembering traumatic life events. Over 100 studies published in peer-reviewed journals show that it is extremely effective at healing the symptoms of anxiety, depression, and PTSD (Research.EFTuniverse.com).

EFT is often called "tapping" because a central feature of EFT involves tapping with your fingertips on acupuncture points on your body. These acupuncture points are referred to as "acupoints." Research has shown that pressure on acupoints, or "acupressure," can be as effective as acupuncture itself (Cherkin et al., 2009). Acupuncture theory teaches that energy flows through our body through pathways called meridians. Disease can be caused by a blockage or interruption of that flow, and acupuncture or acupressure can be used to remove those blockages.

The idea that stimulation of the physical body (also called "somatic stimulation") could play a role in psychological healing arose gradually in the second half of the 20th century. In the 1920s, a colleague of Sigmund Freud, psychiatrist Wilhelm Reich, coined the term "muscular armour" based on his observations that emotional trauma can result in rigidity in certain regions of the body (Reich, 1927). In the 1970s, clinical psychologist Roger Callahan found that clients made rapid shifts in psychological trauma when psychotherapy was combined with tapping on acupressure points (Callahan, 2000). In the 1990s Callahan's method was simplified as EFT and published in a manual (Craig & Fowlie, 1995; Church, 2013).

As EFT became more popular in therapy and coaching circles, it attracted the attention of researchers. They conducted studies of EFT and found that it was extremely effective for mental health problems such as phobias, depression, anxiety, and PTSD (Lane, 2009).

The use of a manual is necessary to ensure that a treatment is applied uniformly from study to study. The Clinical Psychology division of the American Psychological Association (APA) has published guidelines for research. These guidelines determine whether or not a therapy is "empirically validated" (Chambless & Hollon, 1998). There are seven "essential" criteria that are required in order for a study to be considered valid, and one of these is the use of a written manual. This ensures that when a scientific study is replicated, researchers are comparing apples to apples. They are testing the same manualized form of the method that has been tested in other studies. Because *The EFT Manual* was freely available, most of the over 100 studies of EFT were conducted using a uniform version of EFT, which we call Clinical EFT.

A meta-analysis that combined data from 7 randomized controlled trials (RCT) of Clinical EFT for PTSD found that it had a very large treatment effect (Sebastian & Nelms, 2016). On a scale on which 0.5 indicates a moderate effect from a therapy, and 0.8 a large one, EFT had a treatment effect size of 2.96 which is very large indeed. The stories of people who have used EFT for PTSD that I present on the following pages will give you a sense of how radically it transforms the lives of sufferers.

It can take a surprisingly "minor" negative experience to traumatize a child. In a series of studies called the Still Face Experiments, Harvard psychiatrist Edward Tronick examined the effect on a child of a parent's emotional withdrawal (Tronick, Als, Adamson, Wise, & Brazelton, 1979; Tronick, 1989). He instructed the mothers of young babies around 6 months old to keep their faces impassive instead of interacting with their babies.

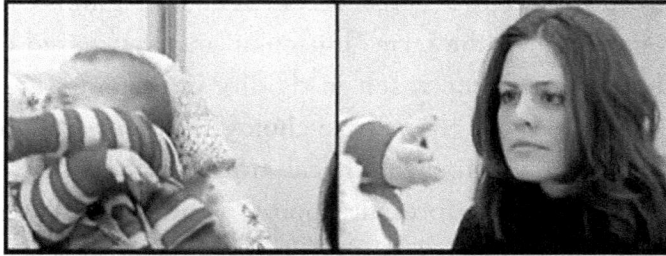

Figure 1. The Still Face Experiments.

When the mothers maintained a still face for a short period, instead of the constant interplay of facial expressions that we unconsciously but continuously use for connection, the babies noticed immediately. If the babies failed to receive facial communication within a minute or two, they became increasingly agitated, then distressed, and finally began to flop around in uncontrolled desperation. While the mother did nothing to harm the baby, the mere withdrawal of connection was sufficient to produce extreme emotional distress.

The phenomenon is not just emotional; it's physiological too. When their emotions are disrupted, their bodies are disrupted as well. "Babies cannot regulate their own emotional states, much less the changes in heart rate, hormone levels, and nervous system activity that accompany emotions" (van der Kolk, 2014, p. 112). They are dependent on cues from the adults around them to produce this regulation. Bonding produces a steady heart rate and a low level of stress hormones. An interruption of connection with their caregivers produces spikes in stress hormones, as well as dysregulation of the nervous system and heart rhythm.

Tronick's work showed that it doesn't take being beaten or abused to affect a young child; the simple absence of emotionally reassuring cues from a caregiver can be traumatic. Sometimes people in my live EFT Level 1 and 2 workshops say, "I grew up in a pretty normal family, I had a happy childhood. So why am I so screwed up?" The answer is that it can take a surprisingly small disconnect from mother or father to upset a young child.

Attachment: Secure vs. Disorganized

During WWII, in order to keep them safe during the Blitz, the rain of bombs dropped on London and other industrial cities, children were often sent away into the countryside and housed with strangers or in group nurseries. A pioneering psychiatrist named John Bowlby was struck by how strongly children were affected by separation from their parents, and began to study the effects of such separation. It occurred in other contexts noted by Bowlby as well, such as boarding schools to which children were often sent at an early age, and hospitals that strictly limited the hours during which parents could visit.

While visiting Regent's Park in London, he noticed that toddlers would venture away from their mothers yet would often look back to make sure they had their attention. When a mother's attention became diverted, perhaps by a friend who stopped by to chat, the child would become anxious and return to the mother (van der Kolk, 2014, p. 111). The mother's attention provided the child with "a secure base" from which to explore the world.

Bowlby noted the same need for connection later described by Tronick. He came to believe that separation produced many of the dysfunctional behaviors that children developed, and laid the foundations of what came to be called "attachment theory."

Children whose needs are attended to by their caregivers develop what's called "secure attachment." Babies communicate their distress directly and immediately when they feel uncomfortable physical sensations such as being hungry, feeling upset, being wet, and feeling tired. When their cries are heard and their needs met, they associate the communication of their needs with getting them met. They learn that it's safe and natural to be tuned in to your body, and aware of your needs.

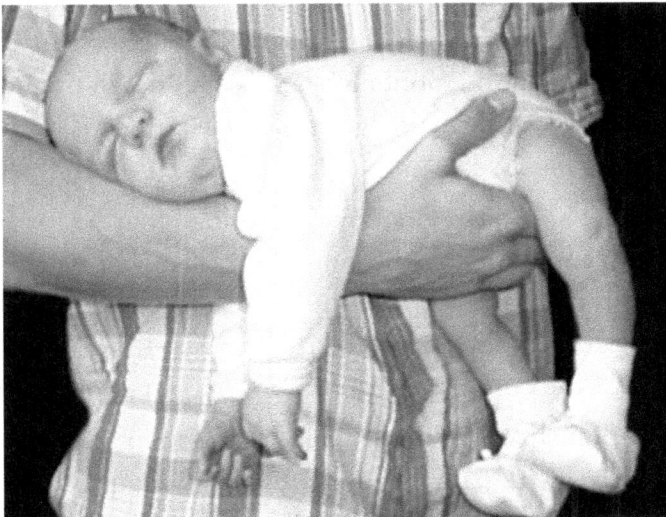

Figure 2. Secure attachment.

Sometimes when I'm in a public place, such as an airport waiting room or grocery store, I'll see a young child with its mother. I enjoy making eye contact with infants, and when I do, they notice immediately. We might smile at each other. I'll make funny faces or noises, and the child might laugh or stare at me curiously. Often the child will bounce, or gesture to indicate that he or she would like me to repeat a particularly amusing grimace. We can have a long dialog with eyes, faces, and body language that requires no words at all.

Babies are exquisitely attuned to the people around them, especially to those few adults with whom they form a primary attachment bond. They read every detail of their faces and body language, and respond accordingly. As a species, being able to attune to the emotions of the people around us gave us an evolutionary edge. Babies who were better at bonding with their caregivers were more likely to survive the many hazards of the Paleolithic era than those that were not. They become synchronized with the people and environment around them. Psychiatrist Bessel van der Kolk, in a brilliant book entitled *The Body Keeps the Score,* calls this the "dance of attunement" (van der Kolk, 2014, p. 111).

Children who don't receive consistent nurturing, or who are ignored or even abused, don't develop secure attachment. Instead they may become anxiously or ambivalently attached, as the parent from whom they're expecting care is unavailable or even a source of pain. They don't develop emotional or physical attunement with those around them, missing the cues that allow people to bond.

Children who are routinely abused or neglected can develop "disorganized attachment." They learn that their crying, pleading, and upset will not produce positive results from their caregiver. No amount of distress they exhibit in response to the physical and emotional signals they're getting from their body (hungry, tired, wet) is sufficient to get their needs met. The caregiver is not attuned to the baby's needs.

The child develops a "deep emotional learning" that his or her needs don't matter. The parent, for the baby the source of nurturing, is also the source of pain. For the baby, the parent is the source of survival, even if they're being abused. According to van der Kolk, "Terror increases the need for attachment, even if the source of the comfort is also the source of terror" (2014, p. 133).

When they're punished for simply expressing their needs, babies begin to associate having needs with pain. They shut down the impulses they're receiving from their bodies in an attempt to avoid punishment. They often develop a sense that there's something wrong with them. No amount of distress they express is enough to make the abuse stop. They become helpless in the face of abuse. This learning is taking place at a body level, long before they develop words, the ability to think consciously, and the brain structures required for cognitive interaction. This type of learning is occurring at the level of the cells, in the deepest layers of the body.

This type of "deep emotional learning" is composed of much more than a summary of what was being experienced through the senses during the original experience. In subconscious implicit memory, it constructs a "mental model of how the world functions, a template or schema that is the individual's sense-making generalization of the raw data of perception and emotion. This model is created and stored with no awareness of doing so. It does not exist in words but is no less well-defined or coherent for that. The emotional brain then uses this model or schema for self-protectively anticipating similar experiences in the future and recognizing them instantly when they begin (or seem) to occur. Emotional memory converts the past into an expectation of the future, without our awareness..." (Ecker, Ticic, & Hulley, 2012).

When their cries are heard and their needs met, babies develop a set of beliefs about the world and attitudes toward nurturing. The first way we learn about self-care is through the care we receive from others, which becomes the template for our subsequent worldview. When children with disorganized attachment become adults, they may have little concept of self-care, and even become self-harming. They believe their needs don't matter, and that their existence is meaningless. They are chronically out of touch with their own bodies, with reduced neural volume in the parts of the brain that govern awareness of the body's location in space (Anderson, Teicher, Polcari, & Renshaw, 2002). The type of PTSD resulting from abuse by a caregiver is a very different matter from PTSD resulting from a single traumatic event in adulthood such as an auto accident. It has been argued that it belongs in its own unique diagnostic category, complex PTSD or C-PTSD, and treatment guidelines for this condition have been developed (Church, Stern, Boath, Stewart, Feinstein, & Clond, 2017).

The Long-Term Results of Disorganized Attachment

The results of disorganized attachment and the dysfunctional lessons learned by such children show up in adulthood. In a 20-year longitudinal study of girls who had been sexually abused, the effects were found to be pervasive (Trickett, Noll, & Putnam, 2011). They had high levels of depression, obesity, dissociation, major illness, and self-mutilation. They entered puberty an average of 18 months earlier than non-abused girls. They had cognitive deficits and abnormal levels of certain hormones. Early in puberty, their levels of androstenedione and testosterone, hormones that stimulate libido, were three to five times higher. Their cortisol responses to stressful events were lower than normal, indicating that their bodies had adapted biochemically to high levels of emotional stress.

Another longitudinal study followed children for 30 years, all the way into adulthood (Sroufe, Egeland, Carlson, & Collins, 2010). It found the quality of early attachment to be the major predictor of adolescent and adult behavior. Children with disorganized attachment were chronically anxious. Not having learned the "dance of attunement" early in life, as adolescents they were unable to regulate their own emotions and had high levels of frustration, aggression, and disruptive behavior.

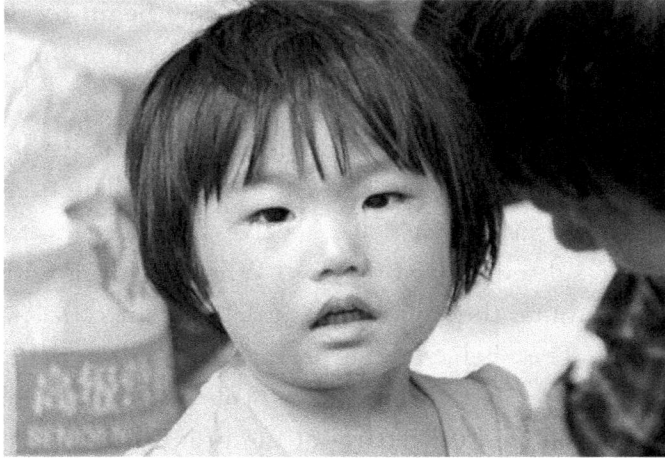

Figure 3. Traumatized child.

They exhibited a lack of empathy for the emotional distress of other people. They failed to develop healthy relationships with peers, caregivers, and teachers. By late adolescence, half of the children in the study had been diagnosed with a mental health condition, and had low levels of resilience, the ability to bounce back after an adverse experience.

Does That Mean My Parent's Lack of Attention Traumatized Me?

Let's now go back to the Still Face Experiments of Edward Tronick. Does this mean that when you failed to pay attention to your baby for 30 minutes, you traumatized her? Does it mean that when your parents were distracted in an otherwise safe and nurturing household, they scarred your psyche for life?

Fortunately, the answer is no. While babies become distressed during the absence of nurturing, most parents quickly return their attention to the child and restore the bonds of connection. Having a "good enough mother" and not a perfect mother is sufficient to produce secure attachment (Winnicott, 1956, pp. 300–305). As they grow older, and experience temporary emotional disconnection in the overall context of attunement, babies gradually learn to regulate their emotions on their own.

Research into attachment theory shows that the majority of children are securely attached and are able to form securely attached relationships as adults (Boris, Fueyo, & Zeanah, 1997). A meta-analysis of two thousand children raised in middle-class households found disorganized attachment in only 15% of cases (Van Ijzendoorn, Schuengel, & Bakermans-Kranenberg, 1999). So your temporary lapses as a parent, and the temporary lapses you experienced as a child, are unlikely to scar you for life, and do not meet any of the criteria for a traumatizing event.

Trauma Is Physical as Well as Psychological

Psychological trauma is not a merely psychological problem; it affects the body at the most fundamental levels. The most basic need of any organism is survival. Other needs, such as digestion, reproduction, and self-actualization, cannot be met if the organism fails to survive. The survival mechanisms of our bodies resulted in the fight-flight-freeze response, and you'll be surprised at how many parts of your life and behavior are driven by this response.

Because survival is essential, when an animal is under threat, every other need and function is recruited to ensure survival. Those physical systems that can assist (such as circulation and respiration) have their functions altered to support survival. Those that are unable to assist (such as reproduction and digestion) are simply shut down. An immediate threat produces a radical reorganization of cellular resources down to the molecular level.

The body's survival functions are controlled by the autonomic nervous system (ANS). At the top of the spinal cord is the hindbrain, the pinnacle of the ANS. It handles all the functions a newborn baby can perform, including excretion, respiration, circulation, and digestion. It continues to perform these functions for adults without any conscious input from the rest of the brain. They happen automatically; for the fancy word "autonomic," you can substitute the straightforward word "automatic" since all these functions are taken care of in a healthy body automatically without any necessity for conscious thought.

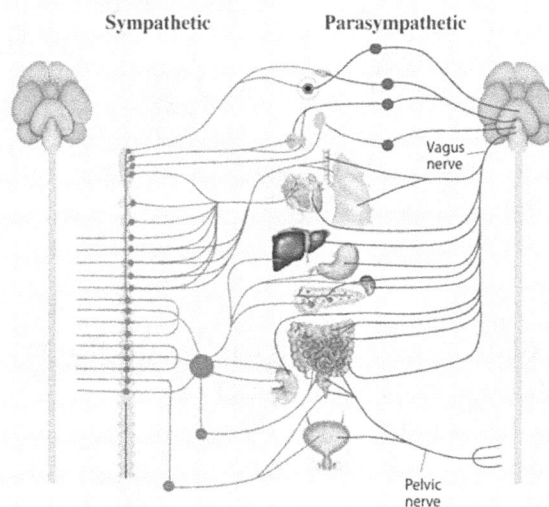

Figure 4. The sympathetic and the parasympathetic
nervous systems.

The ANS has two distinct parts: the sympathetic and the parasympathetic. The sympathetic nervous system (SNS) is responsible for handling stress, while the parasympathetic nervous system (PNS) is responsible for relaxation. When we're stressed, the sympathetic half of the ANS is dominant, and when we're relaxed, the parasympathetic part takes over.

Take a look at the diagram of the sympathetic and parasympathetic systems (Fig. 4), and notice the nerves radiating out from them. They connect with your heart, your lungs, your eyes, your mouth, your digestive system, your liver, your bladder, and your reproductive organs. They're the conductor of the symphony, telling all the systems of your body what to do at any given moment. When you're relaxed, they sound the all-clear, and all your systems go into repair and rejuvenation mode. When you're stressed, they sound the alarm, and all your systems get ready for fight or flight. You can readily observe some of the organs regulated by the ANS when you reflect on the following types of events:

- You have to give a speech. Your mouth dries up. You have knots in your stomach.

- You remember the death of a loved one. You cry.

- You've been working on a project so intently that you forget everything else, and suddenly you're finished and you relax. You have to go to the bathroom.

- Your spouse brings up a dinnertime topic that upsets you. Your food curdles in your stomach.

- A person you despise enters the room. You bristle.

This stress-regulation system has worked so well, for so many millennia, that it's scarcely changed at all. The dinosaurs, extinct for 65 million years, had much the same ANS as you do. So do their descendants, today's lizards and birds. When you're a fetus growing in the womb, this part of your body develops first, just as it does in a salamander or an elephant. The reason that it's changed so little over millions of years is that it was perfected all those ages ago and it's simply so good at doing its job that Mother Nature has had no cause to tinker with it since.

Figure 5 shows the fetuses of various species. You'll see how similar they look at the level of development of the ANS, despite the fact that they will look very different at birth. That's because the ANS is great at its basic survival functions.

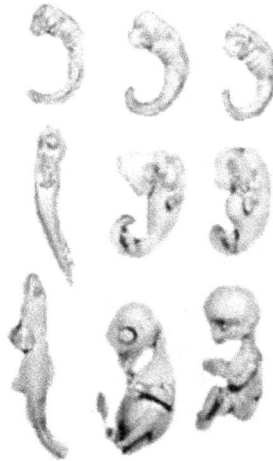

Figure 5. Though they will look very different at maturity, the fetuses of diverse species look remarkably similar early in their development.

The ancient Roman physician Galen first discovered, named, and described the SNS around 170 AD (Swanson, 2014, p. 680). The word "sympathetic" is composed of two parts: *sym*, acting in concert with (as in "symphony"); and *pathos*, or emotion. Galen first observed that the SNS is engaged by emotion. When we're afraid, upset, or angry, it's turned on. It's our neural wiring for responding to threats that engages our emotions. Emotions are not abstract phenomena; through the SNS, they are interwoven with every major organ system of our bodies.

Stress Is Hormonal as Well as Neurological

Neurotransmitters and hormones are molecules that work together with your ANS as a component of the system that signals your body to be stressed or relaxed. The two most important stress hormones are adrenaline and cortisol. Though there are others, I like to use cortisol as shorthand for the whole range of neurochemicals used in response to stress, because it can be measured in saliva and blood and there are many studies showing the stimuli that elevate its levels.

As a convenient shorthand for a relaxation hormone, I use DHEA (dehydroepiandrosterone), because it's your main relaxation hormone. Your body uses it for cell repair and rejuvenation, as well as signaling between cells. When you're stressed, your body makes more cortisol; when relaxed, more DHEA. These hormones move in concert with your SNS and PNS. When your SNS says go into flight or flight, you make lots of cortisol, and shut down production of DHEA. When your SNS says relax, you make lots of DHEA and reduce your production of cortisol. Understanding these cycles is vital to understanding your overall health because of all the body systems—digestion, circulation, reproduction, respiration, and immunity—that are affected by your level of stress and relaxation.

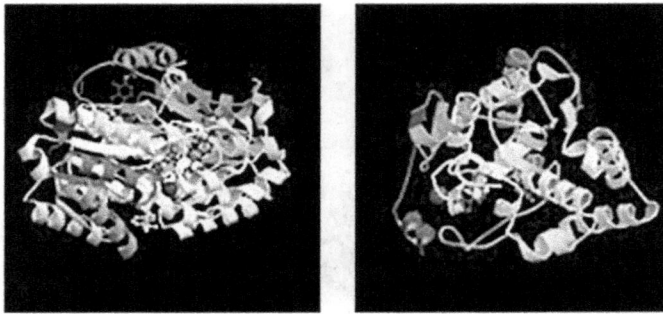

Figure 6. DHEA and cortisol molecules. Notice how similar the two molecules appear. That is because the body synthesizes them from the same precursors.

So if this system is so perfectly adapted to ensuring your survival, how can it be a problem? It's not a problem when children are raised with secure attachment, with periods of slightly elevated stress followed by relaxation and renewed attunement. The dance of attunement develops in the child a somatic or body-based sense of how to manage stress long before it develops the ability to think or reason. These abilities extend to its adult set of competencies.

When children are raised with disorganized attachment, however, they are in high stress mode most of the time. They live with their SNS on continual high alert. They adapt to having the neurophysiology of stress as their "set point." Stress is normal, while relaxation is not. As adults, they tend to have high levels of cortisol and low levels of DHEA. If they are highly stressed for long periods of time, they may deplete their stocks of both hormones, leading to the loss of energy characterized as "adrenal burnout." They may also develop abnormal patterns of cortisol secretion, such as low levels in the morning when cortisol is normally high to give you the energy to start your day, and high cortisol at night. This leads to insomnia and nightmares.

High stress is linked to virtually every type of disease. Studies show chronically high cortisol to be linked to loss of bone density, loss of muscle mass, increased skin wrinkling, cognitive decline, the inability to turn short-term into long-term memories, and many diseases. While a cortisol spike is adaptive when it gives us the shot of juice required to evade danger, it takes a terrible toll on the body if the alarm system is turned on continuously. In traumatized people, it spikes higher and faster, and remains at a high level long after the danger has passed.

Your Body Can't Tell the Difference

Here's the real problem, and how this affects you whether you were raised with secure attachment, disorganized attachment, or anything in between: Your body can't tell the difference between a stressful thought and a stressful event. The subjective stressful thought that's "all in your mind" sends the same signal to your body that an actual objective threat to life and limb produces. Your cortisol shoots up within seconds. Your SNS goes into high alert. All your body systems are affected. You can do this by thought alone, without anything wrong in your environment. You've produced all the neurophysiology of stress in your body while having no objective reason to be on high alert.

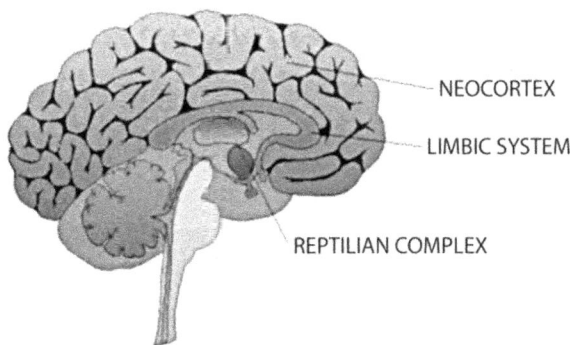

NEOCORTEX

LIMBIC SYSTEM

REPTILIAN COMPLEX

Figure 7. The triune brain.

The human brain has two layers above the reptilian survival system of the ANS. The midbrain or limbic system has many functions, and evolved later. It's the mammalian part of the brain, and it governs emotions. Mammals can feel emotionally in ways that reptiles cannot. They are able to navigate complex webs of social interaction. During the first 18 months after birth, the limbic system is the fastest-growing part of the brain, as the child is learning attachment and attunement. The limbic system creates a map of the world around you. If you grow up attached, your "deep emotional learning" is that the world around you is manageable. The implicit memory systems in our brains make sense of touch, sounds, facial expressions, and other basic forms of contact that are fundamental to a communal species. We learn to regulate our emotions and interact in synchrony with others. Playing with caregivers, friends and siblings, we learn rhythmic patterns of physical coordination that become templates for our future social interactions. The lessons learned during this phase literally become part of the permanent wiring of the brain, which makes them so hard to change later in life.

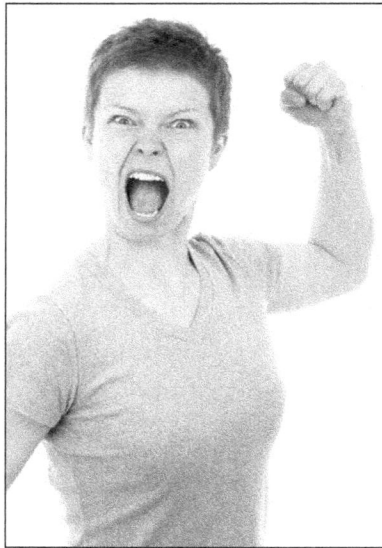

Figure 8. Identifying threatening cues is essential to survival.

Your midbrain also has two structures crucial to the emotional part of the stress response: the hippocampus and the amygdala. The hippocampus is like a military historian. Its job is to examine information coming in from the environment. If it finds a match between a piece of incoming information ("man wearing red shirt") and a previous threat ("I was beaten up when I was 7 by a bully in a red shirt"), it identifies a potential threat in the here and now.

The amygdala is like the fire alarm of the body. Once the hippocampus has made a positive match, and the match is confirmed by other structures in the brain, the amygdala's job is to sound the alarm, telling the SNS to go into fight-or-flight mode.

Driven to Distraction by Your Cortex

Above the mammalian brain is the primate brain, the cortex. This is the part of the brain that monkeys, dolphins, and other highly evolved species possess. It is largest in human beings, who have abilities that non-primates like dogs and cats do not. We're capable of abstract thought. We can reflect on the past, make projections about the future, and create highly structured mental products based on mathematics and poetry. We have language and song. All these are products of the cortex, which in evolutionary terms is the youngest part of the brain.

Where the cortex works against us is when we think abstract thoughts that drive strong emotion and trigger the fight-or-flight response. The thought, "John slammed my ideas at the staff meeting" isn't a threat to your survival, but if you're ruminating on it for hours over the weekend when you should be relaxing, you're driving your cortisol up and your DHEA down. You're engaging your SNS and negating all the cell repair and restoration processes governed by your PNS. There's no threat to your survival—the event happened several days before—yet you're still sending stress signals to your body.

There's a charming Zen story about two celibate monks who were on a long journey. One morning they came to a stream that was in flood. At the bank was a young woman who couldn't get across. The older of the two monks hoisted her onto his broad shoulders, and both monks walked into the water and crossed safely to the other side. After thanking the old monk, the woman went on her way. The two monks walked in silence till dusk, but there was tension in the air, and the dam of emotional intensity in the younger monk eventually burst. "The rules of our religion forbid us to touch women," he said. "How could you have done that?"

"My son," said the older monk, "I picked her up and set her down this morning. You have been carrying her all day."

The angry inner ruminations of the younger monk had been raising his stress level long after the event was over. That's what we do when we obsess about the past or fear for the future. We send stressful messages to our bodies with our thoughts, compromising their ability to regenerate and heal, using the system designed by Mother Nature to be engaged only when we are in true danger.

Your Brain on Trauma

In one study using brain scanning, researchers showed that recalling a past emotional event actually caused those brain regions associated with the visceral physical sensations that we felt during that event to light up (Damasio et al., 2000). Fear produced activation of a different brain region than did happiness.

Brain scans of traumatized people show some interesting patterns even many years after the triggering event (van der Kolk, 2014, p. 42). Unsurprisingly, the amygdala lights up as emotional memories are recalled. But the visual cortex—a structure in the back of the skull that normally processes information from the eyes—also lights up. Even though the person's eyes may be closed, the visual cortex responds as though the person is literally seeing and reexperiencing the event all over again.

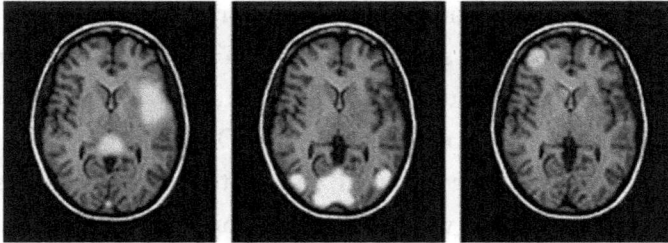

Figure 9. fMRI brain scans. The brain regions activated by trauma: the right side of the limbic system (left), the visual cortex (middle), and deactivation of Broca's speech center (right).

When experiencing or recalling a traumatic event, a section of the brain called Broca's area goes offline. This is the brain center responsible for spoken language. A traumatized person may be feeling all the emotional and physical sensations triggered by a disturbing memory yet be unable to articulate them as this part of the brain shuts down.

Normally, the modern cortical brain functions as a gatekeeper, passing information from the emotional brain through its rational processes. When we hear a loud bang, our hippocampus goes on high alert, but our cortex can reason that it's a car backfiring and not a gunshot, and override the stimulus before a signal is sent to activate the SNS.

Similarly, when we see a box of our favorite chocolates, our cortex can prevent us from seeking immediate gratification by remembering what will happen if we eat them all in one sitting. When we're attracted to a potential lover, our cortex can weigh the long-term advantages and disadvantages of taking action on our sexual desires.

When we're under threat, however, the balance of power between the emotional brain and the reasoning brain changes. It's the job of the emotional brain and SNS to get us out of danger, and it overrides thought. When the ancient emotional brain needs blood for the arms and legs to meet the expected threat, it treats the cortex as no more than a convenient blood supply. The capillaries in the frontal lobes constrict within seconds, forcing blood out of the conscious thinking brain and into the extremities. Up to 70% of the blood drains from the cortex. All your reasoning skills are still encoded in those cortical neurons, but with no blood reaching them they are unavailable to you. Your cortex is like a hard drive with the power turned off. All the information is there, but offline.

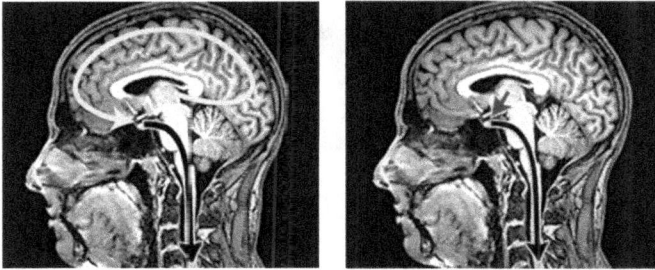

Figure 10. When a normal brain receives sensory input, the limbic system refers it to the neocortex for executive evaluation before signaling the amygdala (left). A PTSD brain takes the short path directly to the amygdala (right).

In people with PTSD, the balance of power between the thinking and emotional brains shifts. They may become enraged at the slightest provocation. They may shrink from normal physical touch. They may overreact to innocuous events. They may perceive the world as full of threats.

Studies of identical male twins, one of whom was drafted into the Vietnam War and the other not, show striking changes in their brains (McNally, 2006). In the twins exposed to combat, the brain regions responsible for memory and learning had shrunk relative to their non-combatant brothers. But the brain pathways tasked with carrying the signals of stress had become hypersensitive, as these had been developed by ongoing survival needs. Though the brains of these twins may have been virtually identical at birth, and before going to war, exposure to trauma led their brains to develop differently as adults.

The brain is constantly adding new connections, a process known as "neurogenesis." It's also pruning old unused circuits. While the ability of the brain to rewire itself in response to experience (this ability is called "neuroplasticity") is of great assistance when we're learning a new skill, it works against us when the circuits we're improving are those associated with stress. Stressed brains reinforce the neural pathways dedicated to carrying stress-related signals, at the expense of the brain regions responsible for memory, learning, and making high-quality executive decisions. Researchers have noted that PTSD symptoms often get worse over time, as neuroplasticity builds up the circuits of stress (Vasterling

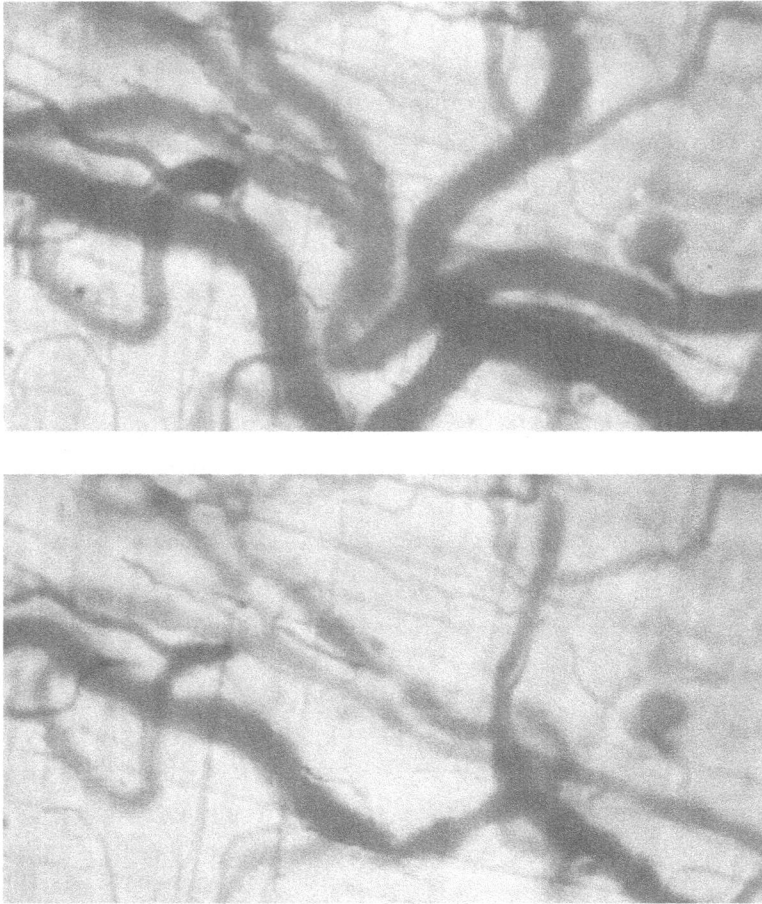

Figure 11. Capillary before and a few seconds after a stress signal.

& Brewin, 2005). In an essay for the journal Energy Psychology, I call this "the dark side of neural plasticity" (Church, 2012).

Over time, PTSD remodels several critical parts of the brain. A study that used fMRI to examine the brains of veterans with PTSD found differences in those who reexperienced the traumatic events of combat more strongly, with flashbacks and intrusive thoughts (Spielberg, McGlinchey, Milberg, & Salat, 2015). The communication between the hippocampus and prefrontal cortex was impaired, making them less able to provide appropriate context to incoming information. The hippocampus was inappropriately sensitive to non-threatening cues.

When a normal brain is confronted with a cue like a group of young men lounging on a street corner, it can make an accurate executive decision about whether they are a threat. A PTSD brain with an overactive hippocampus, receiving identical information, is likely to send a stress signal to the amygdala without first passing it through the executive filters in the cortex. This results in chronic stress.

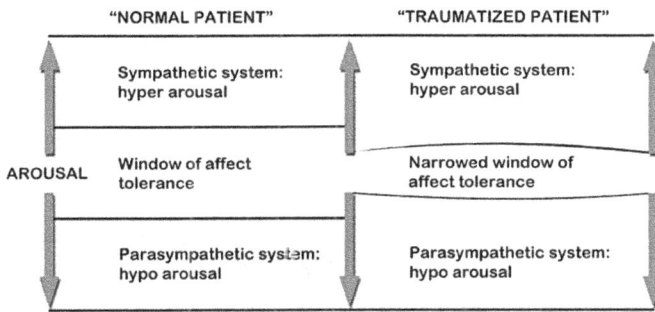

Figure 12. Reaction to stress.

Source: Brodie, E. M. (2015). Dealing with trauma using the non-local mind and shamanic soul retrieval. *Energy Psychology: Theory, Research, and Treatment*, 7(2), 45–56.

In PTSD, the size of the "window" in which a cue is perceived as threatening narrows (see Fig. 12). A smaller number of cues are tagged as non-threatening. The wives of veterans with PTSD often report that small problems that their husbands would shrug off before deployment become triggers for anger and other violent emotions afterward, as their brains become more responsive to stress signals.

These changes in the brain aren't just observed in people with PTSD; people with no psychiatric diagnosis show similar patterns. One study looked at 87 healthy participants and graded their ability to regulate their emotions (Petrovic et al., 2015). Some people had great difficulty dealing with their own anger, irritation, and sadness, and it affected their social, work, and family life. Others did not.

Those who reported the highest levels of negative emotions had smaller amounts of tissue in the orbitofrontal cortex and other brain regions responsible for emotional regulation. Those who had the best emotional regulation also had the most brain tissue in those regions. This shows that hostility, anxiety, depression, and PTSD are not psychiatric diagnoses we either have or don't have. The researchers said that, instead, "there is a continuum in our ability to regulate emotions… such disorders should not be seen as categorical, that you either have the condition or not." Wherever you fall on the spectrum, when you cultivate healthy behaviors, you nudge your neural networks to grow the corresponding parts of the brain.

Bringing the Traumatized Brain Back Online

The brains of people with PTSD do not process information as effectively as normal brains. The parts of the brain are unable to work in synchrony. Normally, all the regions of the brain work together when presented with incoming information. Figure 13 shows the difference (van der Kolk, 2014, p. 311). The PTSD brain has difficulty coordinating its activity in order to process the incoming information, and bring coherent focus to bear on the immediate situation.

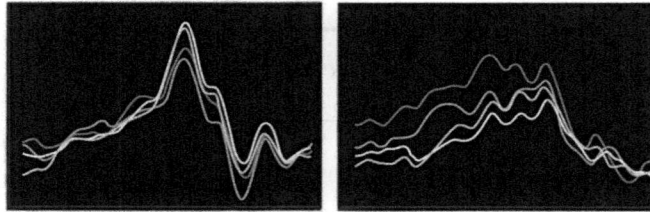

Figure 13. The brains of normal subjects coordinate their functioning to process information (left). The brains of PTSD sufferers aren't able to function in synchrony (right).

A team of EFT volunteers went to Haiti two years after the 2010 earthquake devastated the country and orphaned 250,000 children. They made a 7-minute video showing their work. You can see it at Haiti.EFTuniverse.com. One of the most touching scenes shows "Amelie," a girl who was 8 years old at the time of the earthquake. She and her mother were inside a building that collapsed. Her mother was killed, the girl survived, but it was two days before rescuers pulled Amelie from the rubble. Imagine being trapped and immobilized with your mother's dead body for that length of time. Amelie was so traumatized that she had not spoken a single word in the two years since the earthquake. This is a classic example of the deactivation of Broca's area in the brain. She didn't socialize, laugh, or play with other children her age, indicating that her limbic brain was shut down.

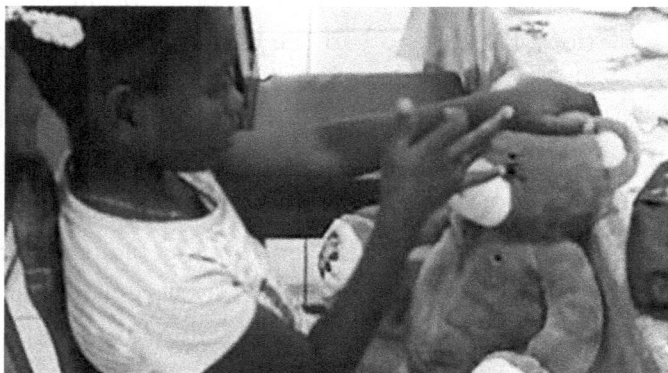

Figure 14. Survivor of the 2010 earthquake in Haiti.

Under the guidance of the EFT practitioners, Amelie taps and starts telling a toy teddy bear how sad she is. After two days, the video shows her laughing and talking and playing with the other kids like a normal child of her age, as Amelie's entire brain comes back online and returns to synchrony.

Reach Out and Touch Someone: The Polyvagal Journey

Though Charles Darwin is best known for his book *The Origin of Species*, late in his life he became fascinated by emotions, and the question of how and why they evolved in the first place. His last book, published in 1872, is called *The Expression of the Emotions in Man and Animals*, and he notes the link between emotions and the stress response, which he calls "escape or avoidance behavior" (Darwin, 1872).

Darwin was struck by the similarities of emotion across species. We can tell immediately if a dog is about to attack, or is relaxed and seeking affection. The language of the body and the many varieties of facial expression are effective in conveying information about the inner emotional states of animals. We are even more sensitive to the emotions of other human beings; for our ancestors, interpreting whether the configuration of hundreds of muscles in the face of a stranger meant "angry, threatening" or "calm, nurturing" meant the difference between life and death. We evolved to be exquisitely tuned to the emotions of those around us.

On a recent telephone coaching call, being broadcast live to a listening audience, my client, a young woman distraught at the recent breakup of her relationship, said the first word, "Hi." I inquired gently, "Are you feeling nervous?"

"Yes," she replied, and we first did EFT on her nervousness at telling her story in front of strangers before we proceeded to work on the issue.

Later, I reflected on the exchange, and wondered how I had known from just a single word that the woman was nervous, and redirected the coaching session to address that. I realized that I had probably heard the tightness in her throat muscles even though I had never heard her utter a word before. I've watched expert psychotherapists also derive a wealth of meaning from the most mundane of small gestures. Gestalt founder Fritz Perls believed that even seemingly mechanical gestures like the tapping of a foot or the raising of an eyebrow were important sources of information.

What is the anatomical basis of this interplay between body and emotions? Darwin believed that the "pneumogastric nerve," which we now call the vagus nerve, played a role in emotional regulation. He wrote that, "Heart, guts and brain communicate intimately via the 'pneumogastric' nerve, the critical nerve involved in the expression and management of emotions in both humans and animals. When the mind is strongly excited, it instantly affects the state of the viscera, so that under excitement there will be much mutual action and reaction between these, the two most important organs of the body" (Darwin, 1872, p. 72)

These prescient observations by a genius of biological science were developed further in the 1980s by Steven Porges of the University of North Carolina. He described the many functions of the vagus nerve and how it ties together emotion and physiological regulation. It connects the brain stem to the tongue, throat, liver, lungs, and all the various organs of the digestive system. It provides a neurological link between emotion and physiological regulation.

Note in Figure 15 all the organs linked to the vagus nerve. Emotions drive all these different physiological systems. When people use common expressions like "I have butterflies in my stomach" and "It takes my breath away" and "I feel it in my bones" and "I felt my heart sink" and "My stomach is churning" and "I have a knot in my stomach" or refer to a "heartfelt" or "gut-wrenching" or "heartbreaking" experience, they are making literal references to the organs engaged by emotion. When we're stressed, our heart pounds, our throat becomes dry, our voice becomes tense, and our breathing becomes shallow. When the stress is due to an interaction with another human being, the emotional experience affects our internal physiological state.

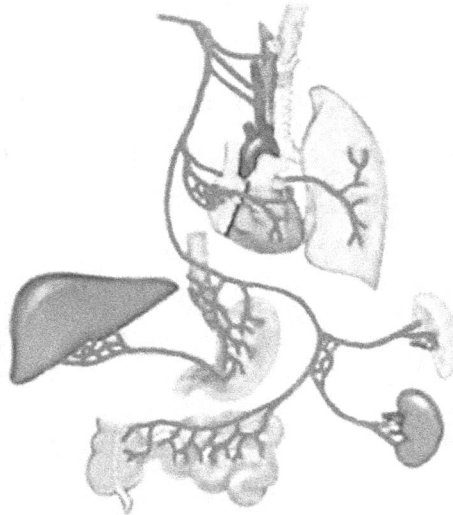

Figure 15. The vagus nerve.

This explains how parents naturally help babies regulate their inner states before they learn to do it themselves. Parents and babies are connected physiologically as well as emotionally and, as Tronick observed, the interruption of emotional connection produces dysregulation of the ANS. The same applies to people in love and to good friends. Emotional connection fosters an innate sense of well-being and physical pleasure, mediated by the vagus nerve. We "feel good" on both an emotional and physiological level when we're interacting with supportive friends and loved ones.

Friends, lovers, and parents also touch each other a great deal; touch is one of the most basic forms in which comfort is communicated (van der Kolk, 2014, p. 218). When we're upset, a friend may hug us or put their arms over our shoulders. Lovers stroke each other's body. Parents wipe away the tears of babies, rock them, stroke their skin, and make soothing noises. When a companion dog or cat is upset, stroking their fur and speaking in a soothing tone of voice calms them down. Soft tones can "soothe a savage breast." Rational reasoning does not send a signal of safety to the brain and body the way touch does.

Porges argues that the many-branched vagal system evolved in response to the increasing social complexity of civilization. The complex anatomy of the vagus shows that we have a great deal of interconnected neurological wiring devoted to being in tune with other people. Each individual is part of a larger dance of attunement, and when large numbers of individuals are closely attuned, they form complex social structures that drive advances in civilization. Darwin regarded this as the opposite of fight or flight, saying that "feeding, shelter and mating activities...are reciprocals of avoidance and escape" (1872, p. 71).

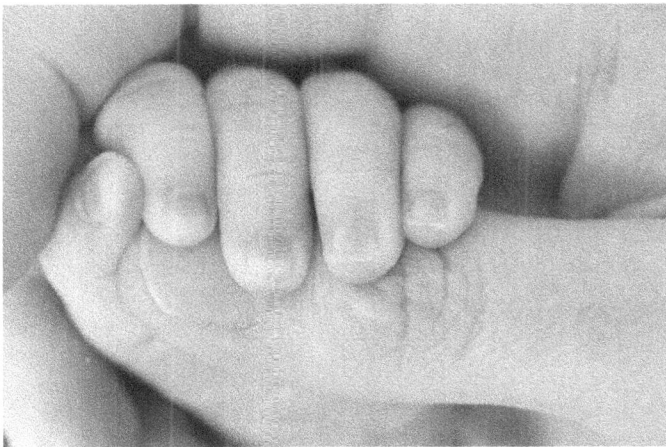

Figure 16. Touch.

The polyvagal theory that Porges developed helps explain why a friendly face or a soothing voice can calm our inner turmoil. Attunement with another person can anchor us when we're feeling upset or alienated from the world around us. We don't have just two ends of a spectrum in the form of fight or flight; social relationships can mediate the stress response. Social engagement is the first level of support to which we instinctively turn when threatened.

Seeking help from others when we're in crisis is a basic human behavior. The first thing we do is turn to others and ask, "Can you help me?" The universal signal of a ship or aircraft in distress is "Mayday, mayday, mayday." This was derived in the 1920s from the French "m'aidez," which means "help me" (Hart, 2012). In a crisis, it is socially acceptable to turn even to complete strangers and ask for help.

If that fails, we go into fight or flight. If that too fails, and we're captured, the vagus nerve again dominates, and shuts down most of our metabolism in the freeze response. For the child trapped by the pedophile priest, the refugee help-less in the face of a natural disaster, the rape victim restrained by her captor, or the warrior pinned down in the foxhole, the freeze response is highly adaptive. The body slows down, awareness dissociates, and consciousness establishes a sense of distance from the source of the trauma by "numbing out."

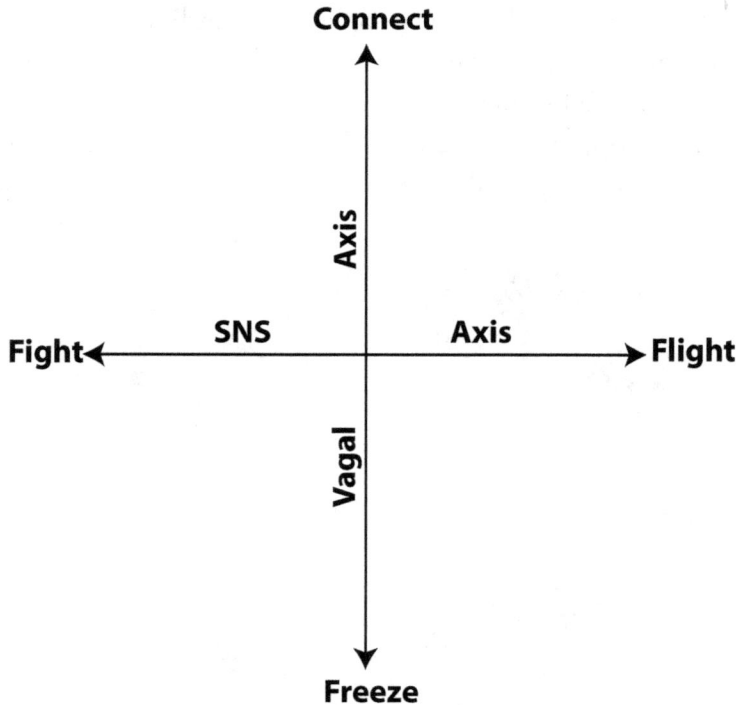

Figure 17. The two axes of the stress response.

Polyvagal theory gives us a more complex understanding of stress than does the simple continuum between fight and flight. That earlier model had just one axis, with "fight" at one end of the SNS spectrum and "flight" at the other. I think of this more sophisticated model as a cross, with the SNS on one axis, and the vagus on the other. Under stress, the top of the vagus axis prompts us to connect. If that fails, we go into fight-or-flight mode. If that too fails, the bottom of the vagus axis protects us using the freeze response.

Polyvagal theory also helps us understand the healing process that can occur after a traumatic event. Numerous studies show that after people have been traumatized, the quality of social connection is one of the most crucial elements in their recovery (van der Kolk, 2014, p. 79). If people have a rich social network, and plenty of support, they are more likely to recover than if their social resources have been shattered.

In one large-scale study I performed with a group of colleagues, we analyzed the PTSD levels of 218 veterans and their spouses (Church & Brooks, 2014). Subjects attended one of six week-long retreats. Being married or coupled was one of the requirements of attendance. They did EFT for their PTSD symptoms in small groups. At the start of the retreats, 83% of the veterans met the criteria for a PTSD diagnosis. By the end, just 7 days later, only 28% did. When they were followed up 6 weeks later, they had maintained their gains ($p < .001$).

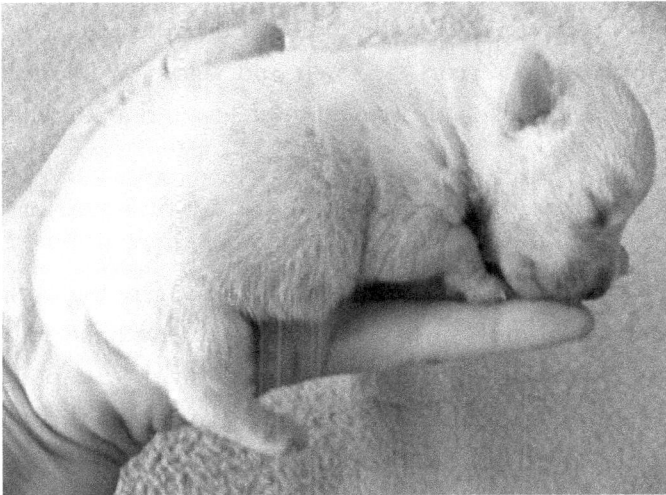

Figure 18. Touch is a universal language that communicates between species.

Living with a veteran with PTSD can by itself be traumatizing, and lead to "transferred PTSD." This phenomenon was evident in the spouses of the veterans in the study. When they began the retreat, 29% of the spouses also met the clinical criteria for PTSD. However, they had results similar to those of their partners. On follow-up, only 4% had diagnosable levels of PTSD. Each of the six retreats was analyzed separately, as though it were a small study by itself. The healing trajectory of participants was the same regardless of which retreat they attended, showing that the results were similar across the different groups. Being with a supportive partner can make a huge difference in the healing process. Social support reinforces the recovery of an individual.

There are a number of stories in *The EFT Manual* (Church, 2013) written by veterans and practitioners who have worked with them. Here is one story by a veteran and another by a psychologist, describing their experiences with EFT.

From a Downward to an Upward Spiral
by Olli

I deployed with 10th Mountain Division, 2nd BCT, to Baghdad from September 2006 through June 2007. I performed a variety of jobs including guard, medical lab, medic, and pharmacy work. My experience was a typical mosaic of long days, stress, and a variety of emotionally powerful events. In short, I was exposed to the following experiences (some face-to-face and others indirectly through my comrades): IED explosions, small arms fire, rocket attacks, sniper attacks, wounded and dead Americans, allies, and Iraqis (military, enemy, and civilians—including women and children), mass casualty, suicide, self-mutilation, divorce, infidelity, fist fights, rape, captured and beheaded U.S. soldiers, imprisoned terrorists, smell and sights of bloody, decomposing, and burnt tissues, booby traps, destroyed vehicles, and a persistent fear of being attacked.

Upon my return from deployment, I began my first year of medical school. Even though I completed the first academic year with good grades, I noticed that my quality of life had diminished significantly. I recognized that I was no longer able to be present in the moment and was always observing whatever was happening in my life from a "witness" perspective. I also replayed many situations in my mind, often thinking of how I could have done them differently. I no longer laughed much and felt burdened by my past, reminiscing my days when ignorance was bliss.

A year went by and I had spoken about my experiences to a variety of people in attempts to "release" them or find peace from their recurrent nature. Talking about the experiences helped me a bit, but only on an intellectual level. I understood that what I was feeling was "a normal reaction to an abnormal situation." I knew that I had done my best and was a force of good in this world. But I also knew that my symptoms persisted even after talking about them. Otherwise I was doing "fine" and identified my symptoms as recurring emotions that were independent of my intellect. They were in a way unreachable, no matter how I tried to resolve or release them. I concluded that this was the price I had to pay, and continued to live my unrewarding life to the best of my ability.

About a month ago I had a powerful experience. I met an old acquaintance who knew me before I deployed to Iraq. Nancy asked if I was open to letting her try something called EFT to help me gain freedom from my recurring emotions. She said it was an "emotional" tool and not a mental one. I agreed and we spent a total of 4 hours doing the work over 2 days. The results were immediate and I literally "fell back" into my body from a defensive posture that I had unknowingly created in my mind. I could feel my body again and could not stop crying and laughing. I could now be present in the moment and not have half of my attention observing the situation as it was happening. I also became less reactive to whistle sounds and sirens that used to initiate in me a fight-or-flight response, as incoming rockets had done in Iraq. Overall, I regained the quality of life that I had prior to deployment.

It was truly an "emotional freedom" technique. Since then, I have been on a constant upward spiral and have been able to transform my past into a great strength. We worked through every single memory and emotion that I was not at peace with and "tapped them out." I also learned how to "self-administer" EFT and have been practicing it on myself whenever something new has emerged from my past.

＊ ＊ ＊

Rather than the downward spiral that so many veterans with PTSD fall into, one that ends in alcoholism, domestic violence, hospitalization, joblessness, or even homelessness, this veteran has now gone on to become a psychiatrist. He has been instrumental in getting EFT to many other veterans suffering from PTSD.

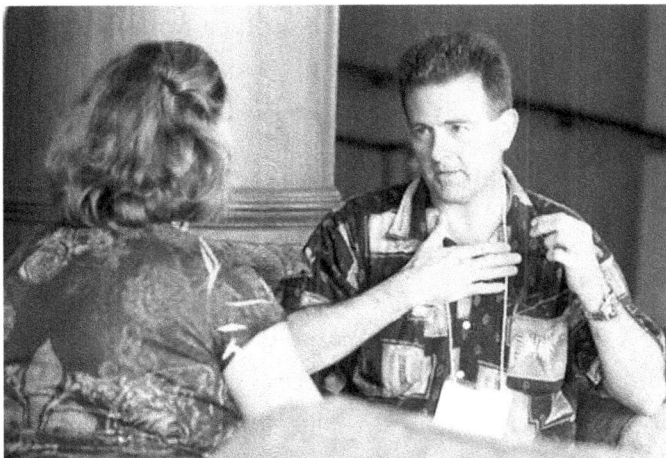

Figure 19. Tapping session with a veteran.

Many therapists have discovered the same effects when they use EFT. Here's an open letter by clinical psychologist Constance Louie-Handelman, PhD, a former captain in the U.S. Army Reserve who was in charge of a forward operating base in Kandahar Province in Afghanistan. She writes how after just one round of EFT tapping, soldiers were noticeably more relieved and calmer.

How EFT Helps Active-Duty Warriors

By Constance Louie-Handelman, PhD, Captain, USAR

I began investigating Emotional Freedom Techniques (EFT) when a friend told me about tapping. Although I have a PhD degree in clinical psychology, I was continually searching for other effective techniques that could help clients. I studied EMDR, neuro-linguistic programming (NLP), and hypnotherapy.

However, after studying and practicing EFT, I found it worked quickly in eliminating fears, limiting beliefs, pain, and releasing traumatic events. Every opportunity I had, I used EFT with family, friends, and clients and achieved excellent long-lasting results. I was so confident in EFT that I felt I had something to offer when I read about the high rate of suicide among U.S. soldiers.

I was commissioned as a captain in the U.S. Army Reserve on March 2010, and was deployed to Afghanistan from July 2011 to May 2012. As a psychologist, I was in charge of a forward operating base in Kandahar Province and officially saw 199 individual soldiers (574 sessions).

Once I established rapport, understood their problems and needs, I used EFT primarily for anger, sleep, depression, and stress.

After just one round of tapping, soldiers were noticeably more relieved and calmer. Soon thereafter, soldiers added more details about their problems, or expressed issues that they had kept to themselves for years. When they felt the profound positive result, it was then easy to encourage soldiers to learn how to tap, something they could do themselves in a matter of minutes, in order to release past, current, or anticipated problems, or "pre-emptive tapping," as one soldier called it.

The ease to learn and to apply the tapping was an important element of EFT since I often saw a solider just for one session.

I realized the success of EFT when soldiers were able to return to full duty, wanting to learn more about EFT, or referring other soldiers to my office. Since returning home, I am disheartened to learn that EFT is not an accepted technique in the U.S. Department of Veterans Affairs (VA). Fortunately, there is the

Veterans Stress Project (www.stressproject.org) that offers free EFT sessions for returning vets.

I can only hope that the VA's powers-that-be will soon realize the effectiveness of EFT in order to help thousands of suffering vets, thus making a dramatic dent in the suicide rate.

❋ ❋ ❋

While Dr. Louie-Handelman's wish for the VA to recognize the effectiveness of EFT hasn't come true yet, progress has been made. When she returned from deployment, she was hired by the San Francisco Veterans Center where she now offers EFT to veterans.

Unresolved Childhood Trauma Becomes Adult Disease

There is an undeniable link between unresolved childhood trauma and adult disease. Though adverse childhood experiences are usually thought of as "emotional" or "psychological," and conditions such as cancer, heart disease, diabetes, and high blood pressure are usually classified as "physiological," the body understands no such distinctions.

In the 1990s, a landmark study was conducted by Kaiser Permanente, a huge hospital chain, in collaboration with the U.S. Centers for Disease Control and Prevention (CDC). Called the Adverse Childhood Experiences (ACE) Study, it examined the health of 17,421 patients at Kaiser hospitals (Felitti et al., 1998). The researchers found that traumatic childhood events were associated with physical disease much later in life. They asked patients whether they had experienced any of 10 traumatic events such as parents who got divorced, were addicts, or suffered from mental illness.

Traumatic childhood events were associated with all the primary adult health risks or diseases including bone fractures, cancer, heart disease, high blood pressure, depression, smoking, suicide, and diabetes. Many other studies have found associations between psychological distress and physiological deterioration (e.g., Belanoff, Kalehzan, Sund, Ficek, & Schatzberg, 2001; Ford & Erlinger, 2004).

Time was not "the great healer" of childhood trauma. The average age of participants in the ACE Study was 57, indicating that the traumatic events that led to disease had occurred half a century earlier. The authors of the ACE Study compared the health care system's focus on treating disease in adults to a fire brigade directing their water at the smoke, rather than at the fire below. They recommend that health care be refocused on treating the emotional traumas that are the source of most "physical" disease. While "psychological" and "physical" might be distinctions that are useful in medicine, the body simply does not make those distinctions.

The Trauma Capsule

What happens when a child experiences an event so disturbing that it cannot be assimilated into ordinary consciousness? Examples of such events might be being beaten for no reason, becoming the object of a parent's sexual desire, hearing harsh unprovoked criticism, or being physically harmed. Children don't understand that such events are not about them, that they are products of the traumatized consciousness of the adults perpetrating them. Unable to escape from their families, without the mental resources to process traumatic events, they often dissociate.

Dissociation is described in the DSM-IV as "...a disruption in the usually integrated functions of consciousness, memory, or perception of the environment" (American Psychiatric Association, 1994). Pain physician Robert Scaer (2012) describes dissociation more practically as a "confused, distracted state in your patient that prevents you from breaking through the fog into any semblance of meaningful contact. It's the patient 'leaving the room' [emotionally] losing contact with you when you've barely touched on the meaningful traumatic material, or when an obtuse reference to some supposedly benign topic causes a short circuit to a traumatic cue in their memory. It's the state of confusion and distraction that the patient describes, as if they've suffered a brain injury."

While dissociation is regarded as a serious obstacle to effective psychological treatment in adults, dissociation can serve a very useful function for an abused or neglected child. Dissociation compartmentalizes the event and allows the child to keep functioning. It wraps the traumatizing event in a capsule. That capsule allows the child to continue existing in the dysfunctional family. In that sense, it's highly adaptive—an essential life skill. Pain physician Robert Scaer (2007) calls it the "dissociative capsule." In EFT workshops, we call it the "trauma capsule." With incomprehensibly terrifying events safely wrapped up in a trauma capsule, the child can continue to function in an inescapable situation.

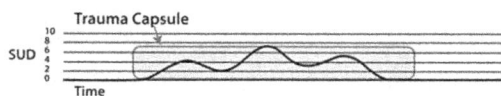

Figure 20. The trauma capsule.

Scaer (2007) observes that the contents of the trauma capsule are frozen in time. The event is encapsulated with all the information from each sensory channel present during the event. The sights, sounds, smells, and feelings of the moment all continue to exist in present tense within the capsule.

When people describe a traumatic event, they often slip into present tense. They describe the event as though it is happening now, not as part of their historical record. In EFT workshops, we train practitioners to be alert for present-tense language because it often indicates that a client is slipping into a trauma capsule. That language is usually packed with emotion, and the client's facial expressions and body postures will change accordingly.

The Adaptive Value of Dissociation

Dissociation may also serve a protective function. For a child who is being physically abused or molested, the body is not a safe space to be. The phenomenon of touch, the most basic of nurturing experiences, becomes a source of terror. Dissociating from the body during acts of abuse can be a coping mechanism, giving the child a sense of psychological distance from the violence.

The accompanying illustration is typical of drawings made by traumatized-people such as incest survivors. The figure of the child cowers, trapped in thecorner and unable to escape. The threatening large figure seems to literally gothrough her body, a symbol of being unable to form boundaries. She has drawn her body without a face. Instead, there's a smiley face up in the corner of the room, a symbol of dissociation. While the shape of the room represents three dimensions, the smiley face is two-dimensional. It's connected to her body only by the line of the room. She has escaped from her violated body into a twodimensional happy-land represented by the face.

Figure 21. Drawing made by an incest victim.

Brain scans of people who are dissociating show that even when recalling highly traumatic events, the emotional centers of their brains are shut down (van der Kolk, 2014, p. 71). Dissociative clients may describe horrifying events with little emotion, the loss of emotional contact described by Scaer. Though this may mean the loss of emotional contact with a therapist or the person to whom the dissociative person is talking, it may go deeper, to the person's loss of contact with his or her body. People who are dissociating may be out of touch with their own bodies, showing none of the physiological signs of stress when recalling traumatic memories. They often have gaps in their memory.

The Thousand-Yard Stare

Dissociation may show up emotionally or psychologically when abused children become adults. They may be out of touch with their emotions, as well as out of touch with their bodies. When attending Harvard Medical School, van der Kolk served as recreational director of the Massachusetts Mental Health Center. He describes basketball games in which patients were "strikingly clumsy and physically uncoordinated" (2014, p. 26). This disorganization extended to their speech; "even their most relaxed conversations seemed stilted, lacking the flow of gestures and facial expressions" that characterize normal social interaction. The traumatized incest survivor of the drawing might dissociate during her adult sexual encounters with men, drifting up into a private space unconnected with her current physical reality.

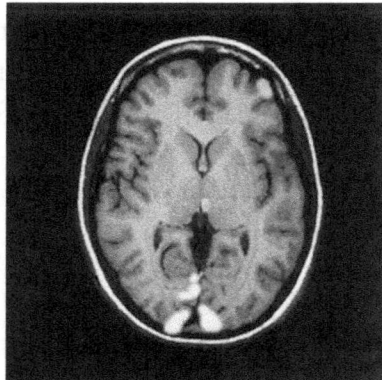

Figure 22. One response to overwhelming trauma is for almost every brain region to shut down. Only a few regions are active.

Adults who have been sexually abused have reduced volume in the cerebellum, a part of the brain responsible for "proprioception," awareness of body's orientation in the space around it (Anderson, Teicher, Polcari, & Renshaw,

2002). The cerebellum coordinates voluntary movements of the body, like balance and posture, and is responsible for smooth and and balanced movement among all the many groups of muscles in the body. Veterans with PTSD also have lower volumes of neural tissue in the cerebellum (Sussman, Wang, Jetly, Dunkley, & Taylor, 2016). As well as veterans, survivors of sexual abuse also have a smaller volume of tissue in the hippocampus, the part of the brain responsible for memory and learning (Frodl, Reinhold, Koutsouleris, Reiser, & Meisenzahl, 2010). They vigilantly scan their environment for threats in the same way that soldiers in combat do (McCrory, De Brito, Sebastian, Mechelli, Bird, Kelly, & Viding, 2011).

Psychologist Jerry Wesch, PhD, former head of the Warrior Combat Stress Reset Program at Fort Hood in Texas, talks about the "thousand-yard stare." When veterans begin talking about a traumatic event, they lose touch with the here and now, break eye contact with the therapist, and go into a private place in their minds. Even though their bodies are safe inside the treatment room with the therapist, their minds are somewhere else entirely. Their heads are inside the trauma capsule reliving all the sights and sounds of the event as though it's happening in the here and now. They've lost touch with the present.

Figure 23. I trained the staff at the Warrior Combat Stress Reset program
at Fort Hood in Clinical EFT.

Veterans have a high level of utilization of medical services. As well as suffering from diagnosable diseases, they have many symptoms that cannot be traced to a medical cause. The research my team did with veterans showed that PTSD is associated with high levels of somaticization—physical symptoms "of unknown etiology" (Church, Hawk, et al., 2013). The sexually abused girls described by Trickett, Noll, and Putnam (2011) also showed deficits of both emotional and physical regulation, with dysregulated hormones, a lack of empathy with the emotional distress of others, poor social relationships, and high rates of engaging in self-harming behaviors such as cutting themselves with razor blades. Their relationships with their emotions, their bodies, and their communities had all become dysfunctional. Traumatized people, having learned that their body is not a safe place to park their identity, take it elsewhere.

While we might classify "physiological" or "medical" symptoms as a physical diagnosis, and "psychological" conditions such as phobias, depression, and PTSD as "mental" ones, they are often two sides of the same coin. Van der Kolk (2014, p. 188) notes that older WWII veterans are more comfortable couching their distress in terms of physical symptoms, while younger veterans of the recent Middle East wars are more comfortable describing their mental health challenges, but these are simply different frames of reference for the experience of traumatization.

Trauma that results from early childhood experiences with caregivers is harder to treat than trauma acquired in adulthood (van der Kolk, 2014, p. 210). For the veteran, the source of trauma is a clearly defined enemy. For the child, the source of trauma is a caregiver, a person who the child expects will nurture and care for them. This violation of expectations at a time when the brain is forming produces very deep emotional wounding. Van der Kolk calls this "developmental trauma," and argues that since it has unique characteristics, it should be included as a new diagnostic category in the DSM.

EFT is unique among therapeutic approaches in that it actually makes deliberate and systematic use of dissociation in the healing process. EFT recognizes that dissociation can perform a protective function. *The EFT Manual* (Church, 2013) describes three "Gentle Techniques" for working on events so traumatic they cannot be approached in ordinary states of consciousness. The three Gentle Techniques allow the client to dissociate just enough to feel safe, while also tapping. This creates enough psychological distance from the event to allow the client to begin the healing process. The felt sense of safety engendered by the Gentle Techniques quickly demonstrates to the client that it may be possible to reduce the degree of emotional triggering around the event. With this encouragement, the client then approaches the event at his or her own pace, dissociating less and less until he or she is able to tap on the memory itself without dissociation.

One of those techniques, called "Tearless Trauma," allows clients to introduce as many layers of dissociation between themselves and the event as they desire. I was working with one client at an EFT workshop who had been sexually molested when she was 2 years old. The traumatic events of "Susie's" childhood had affected her sexual relationships as an adult. She said "I have this concrete barrier at my waist that cuts off everything below."

She could not bear to think of the event, so she put the event "in a box" with eight padlocks sealing it shut. That still wasn't a safe enough distance, so we put the box inside a safe with thick metal walls. We put the safe inside a bank vault. I asked if Susie wanted the bank to be located on the other side of the country, and she said, "No, the bank is on Mars." Only when the traumatic event was inside a box, inside a safe, inside a vault, on another planet, did she feel safe. We used a scale ranging from 0 (no distress) to 10 (maximum distress) to assess her fear (Wolpe, 1958). With the bank on Mars, she was 3 out of 10.

We began to tap, and Susie's distress rating went down to 0. When we brought the bank from Mars to Earth, she was back at an 8, so we tapped till she was at 0 again. Then we took the safe out of the vault, and she was back up at a 10 as the protective dissociative barrier disappeared. We tapped till she was at 0 again, after which she took the box out of the safe.

Tapping again brought Susie to a 0, and then she was ready to open the padlocks. With those removed, she was again at a 10, but EFT quickly brought her down to the point where she was at last ready to open the box. She opened the box, went up to an 8, and we tapped on the event itself. Eventually, it went down to 0. I then asked her about the concrete barrier around her waist. She responded, "It turned into sea sand, and then blew away in the wind."

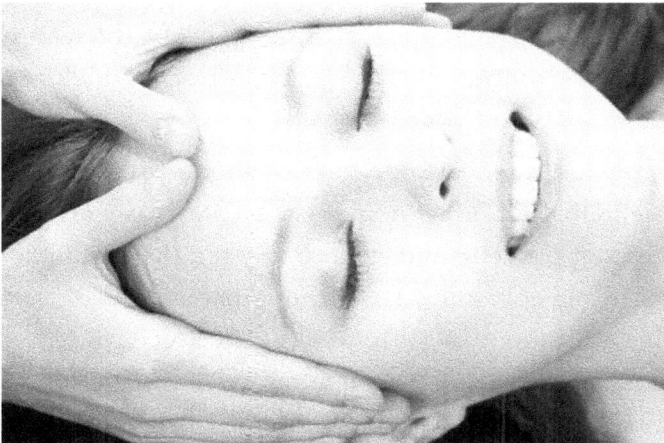

Figure 24. Pressure on acupoints can be as effective as needling.

Tearless Trauma gave Susie multiple layers of safety between herself and the event. We used dissociation deliberately to give her enough distance from the trauma to begin to work on it. It was not a "one-minute wonder," as often occurs with EFT; the session took about 45 minutes. But it allowed Susie to resolve a childhood trauma around which her whole life had previously pivoted. She approached it at her own pace, with as many levels of distance as she required to feel safe. As her coach, I was little more than a guide, simply following her lead and using EFT on whatever target she presented.

When a traumatic memory has been successfully resolved, the client will spontaneously begin referring to it in the past tense. It's now become part of their history, not their present. The client's emotional language and body postures will reflect the change. Resolution can be seen in cognitive shifts, as they perceive the event differently. They're reporting the event from a place of psychological safety, not acting as though the event is an immediate threat to their physical survival. It's correctly perceived as being in the past, rather than inappropriately perceived as being in the present. Susie goes from describing the concrete barrier around her waist as being in the present tense, to the sand having blown away in the wind in the past tense. Cognitive shifts such as changes in tense are vital clues to the progress of the healing process.

Stroking Your Inner Dog

Tapping on acupuncture points soothes the body. It sends a signal of safety to the emotional brain that counteracts the signal of stress coming from a traumatic memory. MRI studies show that acupuncture shuts down the brain's fear centers, regulating an overstimulated amygdala (Napadow et al., 2007; Hui et al., 2005; Fang et al., 2009). It speaks to the parts of the brain that respond to touch and other sensory input, not to the neocortex in which reason resides. For this reason I call it "stroking your inner dog."

Acupressure helps dissociated people feel safe in their bodies, sometimes for the first time. This provides them with a base of security from which they can begin the healing process, and start to unpack their trauma capsules, just as Susie did. Randomized controlled trials show that as well as successfully treating PTSD symptoms in traumatized veterans, EFT reduces the symptoms of "somatization," the array of baffling physical ailments that have no medically discernible cause (Church, Hawk, et al., 2013; Geronilla, McWilliams, & Clond, 2014).

One of the three Gentle Techniques is specifically aimed at physical symptoms. It's called Chasing the Pain, and it is effective for clients who are uncomfortable talking about their emotions, but are very ready to describe their physical symptoms. Veterans in general and older veterans in particular are notoriously reluctant to discuss their mental health problems, but will readily describe physical symptoms: these are "medical" and "objective" and don't carry the perceived stigma that "emotional problems" do (van der Kolk, 2014, p. 19).

PTSD, Anxiety, and Depression as Chemical Imbalances in the Brain

Over the past century, physiologists have made many exciting discoveries about the body. The first hormone to be discovered was adrenaline (epinephrine) in 1900. In 1921, the first neurotransmitter, acetylcholine, was identified. As more of these essential protein molecules were discovered, and their link to human emotions understood, the race to find drugs that might modify their action began.

Pharmaceutical drugs have produced unparalleled improvements in human health in the past 150 years. Imagine a world before antibiotics or painkillers. However, because drugs have worked spectacularly well for certain conditions such as infectious diseases, the drug model has come to dominate medicine, displacing personal self-efficacy and non-pharmacological approaches such as psychotherapy and natural remedies.

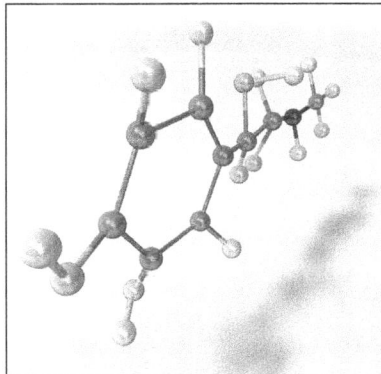

Figure 25. Adrenaline molecule.

My wife and I saw a 20-something woman tanning in the sun a few years back. "Aren't you afraid of skin cancer?" my wife asked her. She shrugged and said, "Soon the doctors will have a pill that will handle it." She was so confident in as-yet-undiscovered miracle cures that she was willing to bet her health on them, abdicating responsibility for her own well-being in the present, and handing it over to imaginary doctors of the future who would produce a magical cure for the results of her own self-neglect.

The biomedical model has come to dominate the popular imagination, as well as the professions of medicine and psychology. In the mid 20th century, psychotherapy was the way most mental illness was treated. Today psychotherapy has been displaced by drug therapies. Human brain function is regarded as a matter of chemistry rather than choice or behavior. A standard textbook declared: "The cause of mental illness is now considered an aberration of the brain, a chemical imbalance" (Deacon & Lickel, 2009).

However, the limits of this approach have become painfully obvious. Today prescription painkillers kill more people each year than guns or car accidents (van der Kolk, 2014, p. 349). While the cautious and appropriate prescribing of antidepressants and other psychotropic drugs can help certain patients, these drugs are being prescribed far more broadly than the scientific evidence supports.

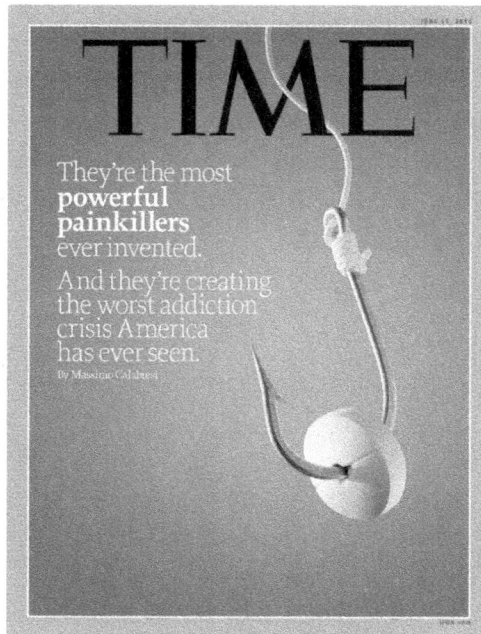

Figure 26. *Time* magazine—the painful cost of painkillers.

Because the number of prescriptions written for antidepressant drugs has soared, you would imagine that rates of depression should have plummeted. The opposite is true. The number of people diagnosed with depression has doubled in the past decade (Hidaka, 2012). In his book *Anatomy of an Epidemic,* medical journalist Robert Whitaker outlines the research showing that many of these drugs have serious side effects, and that long-term use of antidepressants may actually cause chronic depression by disrupting the normal functioning of the brain (Whitaker, 2011).

The VA Could Have Remediated PTSD for Half the Cost of One Drug

During the first decade of this century, the U.S. Veterans Administration (VA) and the Department of Defense (DOD) spent $791 million on a drug called risperidone (Tal, 2013). Initially touted as a treatment for PTSD, a clinical trial published in the *Journal of the American Medical Association* eventually showed that it was no more effective than a placebo, an inert comparison pill (Krystal et al., 2011).

Because they offer the allure of a quick fix, writing prescriptions for PTSD and other mental health problems such as anxiety and depression has become the norm in the military. Meanwhile, the Pentagon and VA rebuffed repeated attempts to evaluate EFT, an evidence-based behavioral treatment, for PTSD. EFT studies were presented to the VA as early as 2008, when Senator Carl Levin, chair of the Senate Veterans Affairs Committee, wrote a personal letter to Secretary for Veterans Affairs Eric Shinseki, enclosing an early outcome study showing veterans recovering from PTSD after EFT treatment (Church, Geronilla, & Dinter, 2009).

Top drug sales

Top drug sales estimates for military and retail pharmacies, 2002-2011

Brand	Combined sales
Lipitor	$1,317,000,000
Plavix	$1,317,000,000
Advair	$1,148,000,000
Nexium	$983,000,000
Singulair	$973,000,000
Celebrex	$903,000,000
Zocor	$781,000,000
Prevacid	$670,000,000
Aciphex	$664,000,000
Actos	$613,000,000
Enbrel	$594,000,000
Effexor	$494,000,000
Fosamax	$481,000,000
Ambien	$417,000,000
Zyrtec	$413,000,000

Sources: TRICARE; Defense Logistics Agency

Figure 27. Military sales of top prescription drugs.

Three other congressmen wrote to Shinseki again in 2010, enclosing more research and further evidence. They proposed seven simple and cost-free steps to help veterans gain access to EFT, such as circulating copies of clinical trials to VA mental health professionals. None of these steps was taken. In September 2013, Congressman Tim Ryan (D-Ohio) wrote another letter to Secretary Shinseki, this time advocating EFT on the basis of 11 clinical trials. Like all the other letters, this one was rebuffed, with the VA declining to examine the evidence, perform its own research, refer patients to the Veterans Stress Project, or take any other action to get EFT to suffering veterans.

The costs of such failure are staggering. Each veteran with PTSD costs an estimated $1.4 million to treat (Kanter, 2007). The cumulative cost to society of treating both the remaining 400,000 Vietnam veterans with PTSD, as well as the estimated 500,000 PTSD-afflicted veterans of the recent Middle East wars, exceeds $1 trillion (Church, 2014). By way of contrast, the cost of six sessions with an EFT practitioner for every one of these veterans comes to $300 million. For less than half of what the military spent on risperidone, it could have purchased this effective and safe behavioral treatment for every veteran with PTSD. If the results were as good as those in the studies, nearly nine out of 10 of those veterans would be PTSD-free today.

Meanwhile, the prescription drug machine rolls on. In 2012, according to an investigative report in the *American-Statesman,* "the Pentagon spent more on pills, injections and vaccines than it did on Black Hawk helicopters, Abrams tanks,

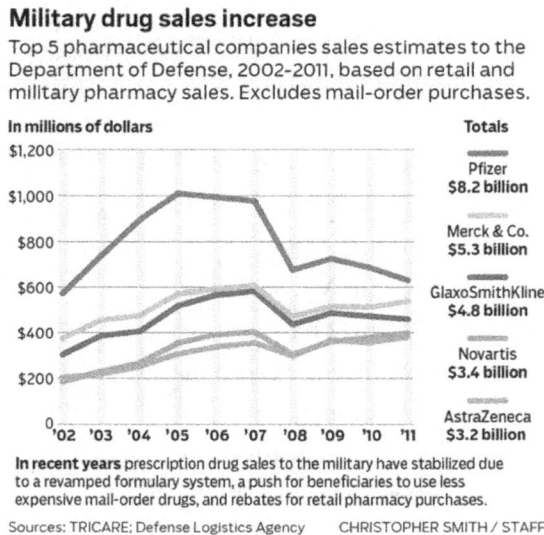

Military drug sales increase

Top 5 pharmaceutical companies sales estimates to the Department of Defense, 2002-2011, based on retail and military pharmacy sales. Excludes mail-order purchases.

In millions of dollars

Totals

Pfizer $8.2 billion

Merck & Co. $5.3 billion

GlaxoSmithKline $4.8 billion

Novartis $3.4 billion

AstraZeneca $3.2 billion

In recent years prescription drug sales to the military have stabilized due to a revamped formulary system, a push for beneficiaries to use less expensive mail-order drugs, and rebates for retail pharmacy purchases.

Sources: TRICARE; Defense Logistics Agency   CHRISTOPHER SMITH / STAFF

Figure 28. Increasing revenue to Big Pharma from military sales.

Hercules C-130 cargo planes and Patriot missiles—combined" (Smith, 2012).

The widespread belief that there's a pill for everything leads both individuals and governments to seek medical solutions to problems instead of empowered personal action. Although our modern society has an impressive array of medical resources, they are not a substitute for self-care. Responsibility for our well-being rests on our own shoulders as individuals, and is not in the hands of our doctors and psychologists. They're there to support our health, not to magically fix us. Through practices such as yoga, mindfulness, relaxation, and EFT, we can regulate our own physiology, including neurotransmitters, hormones, genes and brain waves. No prescription is required.

Meditate Like a Master

An ordered body can regulate a disordered mind. Over 80% of the nerve fibers in the vagus nerve are "afferent," meaning that they run from the body to the brain rather than vice versa. Ancient practices such as yoga and qigong have practitioners regulate their breathing to produce a calm mind; the body postures of hatha yoga were originally developed as a prelude to meditation. When we consciously and deliberately engage in practices that produce physical calmness, we signal the limbic brain that we're safe at a physiological level.

In 2008, I traveled widely offering keynote speeches to share the ideas in my book *The Genie in Your Genes*. I had a series of discussions with scientists about these practices of physiological regulation and why they were so effective at addressing mental health challenges such as anxiety and depression. I had also begun meditating every morning a few years earlier.

As I studied the physiological states of meditation masters, I realized that they have common characteristics. In deep meditation, the beta waves that characterize normal brain functioning disappear, as well as the high-frequency beta that is the signature brain wave of anxiety. Alpha waves, associated with relaxed alertness, are present. The two slowest brain waves, theta and delta, which predominate in sleep, hypnosis, trance, and superlearning states, increase in amplitude. Theta is also the dominant wave of healers when they are offering healing sessions to their clients (Beck, 1986). The fastest of all brain waves is gamma, which is associated with flashes of insight that coordinate information from many brain regions simultaneously.

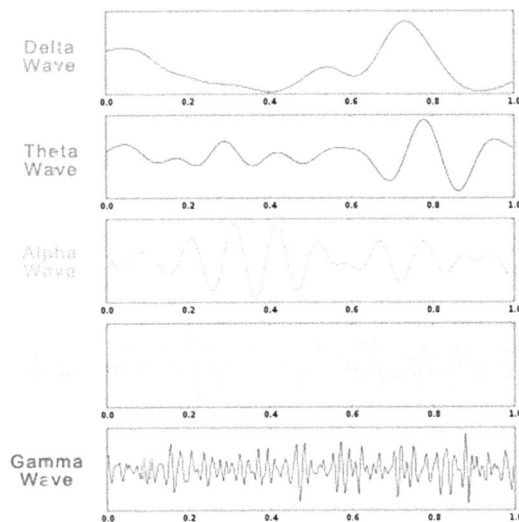

Figure 29. Brain waves.

In deep meditation, the ANS is in relaxation mode, with PNS activity predominating. I also learned the heart coherence techniques taught by the HeartMath institute. When I hooked meditators up to a heart coherence monitor, I discovered that they are usually not in heart coherence. However, they can be trained to enter and maintain heart coherence while meditating. Ancient practices such as the Ujjai breath taught in yoga automatically put people into heart coherence and signal the ANS to enter relaxation mode.

I combined these with practices from neurofeedback and began teaching the package as a form of meditation. Called EcoMeditation, it dispenses with all the spiritual teachings and belief systems that usually accompany meditation. It simply has people enter the physiological state of a meditation master by replicating the breathing, heart coherence, physical posture, and brain-wave characteristics of a master. This is very easy to do and entering this state takes only about 90 seconds. It requires no training whatsoever and the instructions are only a page long (EcoMeditation.com).

I have now taught EcoMeditation to thousands of people, most of whom have tried meditation in the past but found it too difficult to practice regularly. In 90 seconds, a whole roomful of people will be in heart coherence, relaxed, with PNS activity predominating. Theta waves will predominate in their brains, with some alpha and delta remaining. After the 90-second induction period, I have them remain in that state for 15 to 20 minutes, then return their attention to the environment around them. The whole process takes under half an hour and I structure the experience to demonstrate that having a regular meditation practice need not be difficult and does not require much time. Once they learn such self-regulation, and notice how good their bodies feel, they are often motivated to make it a regular part of their day. Such self-care is within the grasp of virtually anyone.

A study of participants at an EcoMeditation workshop found positive changes in many markers of their health. Cortisol was significantly reduced, while levels of a primary marker of immunity called Salivary Immunoglobulin A rose sharply (Bach, Groesbeck, Stapleton, Banton, Blickheuser, & Church, 2016). This increased physiological regulation corresponded to significant improvements in mental health. The symptoms of anxiety, depression and PTSD reduced, as well as physical pain. When the researchers performed later follow-ups with participants, they found that they'd maintained most of their gains.

When we practice responsible self-care, we're far less likely to require medical intervention. Postsurgical recovery times for fit and healthy people are much shorter. When we do have a crisis that requires medical intervention, we have a marvelous array of modern drugs and surgical techniques available to us, giving us the best of both worlds. Self-care and good medicine are both essential; neither excludes the other.

What Approaches Really Work with PTSD?

One of my medical heroes is a psychiatrist named Joseph Wolpe. Though nearly forgotten today, he was one of the most influential figures in psychology in the middle of the 20th century. After WWII he treated hundreds of veterans with "shell shock," the official name for combat trauma before the diagnosis of PTSD was developed.

Though trained as a Freudian, he quickly became disillusioned with psychoanalysis. He noticed that "the talking cure" didn't work with shell-shocked veterans. They often became more distraught by talking about their experiences, as they relived horrifying events. After the Vietnam War, psychologist Charles Figley christened this phenomenon "retraumatization" (Figley, 1986). Recalling a traumatic event can set up the same neurophysiological responses evoked by the original event. As the neural circuits engaged during the original event are activated, the process of neurogenesis commences, and the neural bundles that carry those signals are enhanced. Wolpe went so far as to say that, for a traumatized person, talking about the event was worse than useless; it was harmful.

As well as shattering combat memories, early childhood trauma is encoded deep in the neural network. The brains of babies show a predominance of delta waves, just like the states of deep sleep, superlearning, trance, and hypnosis (Lipton, 2008). Newborns sleep most of the day, only emerging from delta for brief periods of time. They then develop theta, which predominates from the age of 2 to 5 years (Geary & Huffman, 2002). Theta is the characteristic state of rapid eye movement (REM) sleep, in which the most vivid dreams occur, and delta of non-REM sleep. Theta is also the dominant wave during hypnosis, trance, meditation, creativity, tranquility, and feeling "in the zone." From the age of 6 to 12 years, alpha waves predominate, and from then on, beta, the wave characteristic of our conscious thinking brain.

These developmental stages of brain function have profound implications for the understanding of trauma. When a child in theta and delta is subjected to traumatizing events, they don't have the cognitive capacity to reason or cope with the experience. With the brain in a superlearning trance state, these memory tracks are laid down at a preverbal level. This emotional learning is deeply embedded in neural circuits formed early in life and reinforced by neural plasticity. They are difficult to treat later on, since they are so strongly conditioned, as well as having been formed prior to the acquisition of language.

During the first 18 months of life, the limbic system is the fastest-growing region of the brain. It's also the part of the brain that governs social connectivity. When a young child has experiences with a caregiver that lead to disorganized attachment, they are embedded in the growing limbic system and shape the subsequent brain functioning of that person as an adult.

While cognitive therapies or the verbal component of EFT may be successful for treating traumas experienced later in childhood, they have difficulty reaching these early traumas experienced before the development of the cognitive functions carried out by the brain in an alpha and beta state. Lessons about safety, security, relationship, and attachment that are learned during the theta-delta superlearning trance of early childhood are almost impossible to unlearn later. They shape the worldview and brain of an individual for his or her entire life, creating a neurological lens through which all subsequent experience is viewed. A shattering adult experience such as war can also lead to deep emotional learning and the subsequent brain dysregulation characteristic of PTSD.

Wolpe experimented with many different approaches in a creative attempt to "countercondition" the conditioned responses his veterans had to stressful memories. What he eventually discovered was most successful was diaphragmatic breathing. Veterans would focus on breathing while remembering the event, and the pairing of breathing and memory was often enough to neutralize the emotional impact of the memory. Wolpe designed the simple yet elegant scale that we use in EFT, called Subjective Units of Distress or SUD (Wolpe, 1958). People were instructed to rate their degree of emotional distress from 0, no distress, to 10, maximum possible distress, when remembering the event. A drop in the score meant that the treatment was succeeding.

Staying in the Body

Getting SUD scores every few minutes also encourages clients to stay tuned in to their bodies. Van der Kolk regards getting veterans "back into their bodies" to be one of the hallmarks of successful treatment (2014, p. 47). Another is bringing them back into the present moment. When they were traumatized, they learned how to escape the horror they were experiencing by dissociating, with awareness escaping from the here and now. Effective treatments put them back in touch with their physical sensations, and the reality of what's happening in the present.

Acupoint tapping wasn't practiced in the West during Wolpe's time, but EFT still uses the same SUD testing method, the same focus on the present moment, and the same body awareness. What Wolpe's diaphragmatic breathing and EFT have in common is that they keep the client from dissociating by maintaining a firm focus on the physical present. Other effective therapies such as Eye Movement Desensitization and Reprocessing (EMDR) and Somatic Experiencing do the same thing. They keep the client in the present moment, and in their body, while recalling a past trauma.

In all these therapeutic approaches, the immediate experience of physical safety effectively counterconditions the old stress response. Even though the traumatized person is thinking of a stressful event, these body-focused approaches remind them that they're safe in the here and now. This breaks the association in the brain's limbic system between the stressful memory and the fight-or-flight response. Once the association is broken one time, it's usually broken for good. That's why long-term studies that follow participants long after their EFT therapy sessions are over find that their recovery is permanent.

Talk therapy can be effective, and some approaches such as cognitive behavior therapy have a long track record of success. For traumatized people, however, talking about their issues can retraumatize them. In a large study of veterans diagnosed with PTSD and enrolled in a care program at a VA hospital, nine out of 10 did not complete the required program (Seal et al., 2010). We've heard this from many veterans who've been through our six-session EFT program at the Veterans Stress Project after dropping out of VA programs. They make statements like "Talking about the war just made me feel worse." In a study of cognitive behavioral therapy for PTSD, half the participants did not respond to treatment (Monson et al., 2006), in contrast to EFT studies that show upward of 80% veterans permanently rehabilitated.

Reducing Stress Hormones

In 2005, I had a striking experience while watching a group of trainee EFT practitioners. I was astonished at their incompetence. They were missing obvious physical cues from their clients, such as deep sighs and relaxing shoulders. They were missing verbal cues such as changes in psychological perspective, forgiveness, and acceptance. They didn't know the exact location of the acupressure points, and they were often tapping far off the mark. They were trying too hard to bring SUD scores down, instead of following and validating the client's experience. They were applying EFT techniques mechanically rather than organically. All of these mistakes were understandable on their learning curve.

What struck me forcibly, however, was that despite the shortcomings of the practitioners, the clients were getting results. They weren't getting results as good as they might have obtained from working with an expert practitioner, but they were getting results far better than those I'd seen in my earlier training in Gestalt therapy.

As I watched clients physically relax, I wondered what might be happening invisibly inside their bodies to their stress hormones. To answer this research question, I designed a study to examine their cortisol levels. With colleagues from the California Pacific Medical Center and the University of Arizona, I conducted the first study that examined both psychological conditions such as anxiety and depression, and cortisol levels before and after EFT (Church, Yount, & Brooks, 2012).

The study was ambitious and took several years to complete. It was conducted at five integrative medical clinics in California, and eventually included 83 subjects. It was a triple-blind randomized controlled trial, the highest standard of scientific proof. The results were remarkable, and the study was published in a prestigious journal, the oldest peer-reviewed psychiatry journal in North America.

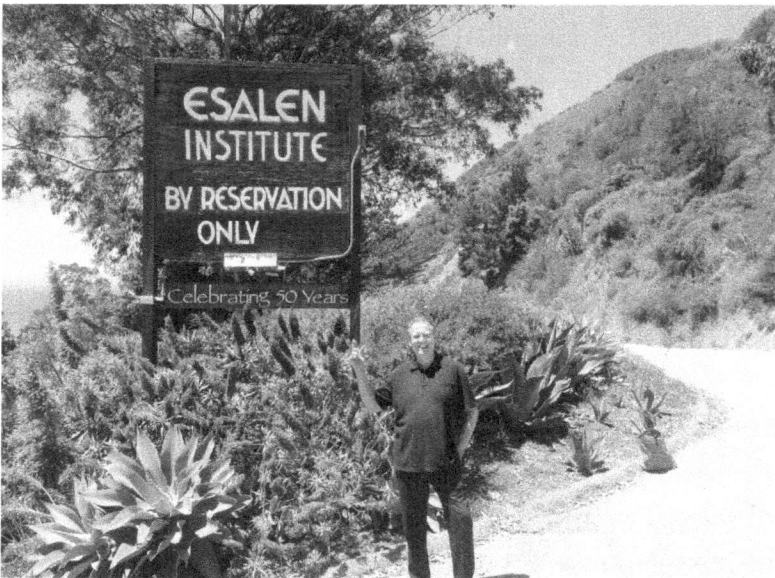

Figure 30. Esalen Institute front gate.

We assessed subjects' mental health, and also measured their cortisol, before and after a single therapy session. One group received EFT, a second group talk therapy, and a third group simply rested. Psychological symptoms such as anxiety and depression declined in the talk therapy and rest groups, but they dropped more than twice as much in the EFT group. Cortisol dropped quickly and significantly. The study showed that EFT was having an effect inside the body.

Later, I had the opportunity to find out just what's happening inside the bodies of people taking an EFT Level 1 and 2 workshop. This particular workshop was held at California's Esalen Institute, the place where Gestalt therapy, Rolfing, Humanistic Psychology, and many other groundbreaking approaches were first developed.

The research team measured a comprehensive panel of physiological markers, as well as psychological conditions like anxiety, depression and PTSD (Groesbeck, Bach, Stapleton, Banton, Blickheuser, & Church, 2016). As anticipated, large improvements in mental health occurred during the week. However, the changes in physiological markers of health were extraordinary. Cortisol dropped by 49%. Salivary Immunoglobulin A rose by 61%. Resting heart rate dropped by 8%, while blood pressure was reduced by 6%. The blood pressure, cortisol and heart rate figures showed that participants were markedly less stressed at the end of the week than the beginning.

While an hour of EFT had reduced cortisol by 24% in the previous study, a week of tapping was associated with an even bigger stress-reduction effect. Participant pain dropped by 66%, while happiness increased by 13%. When follow-ups for psychological symptoms were performed a few months later, most of the improvements held. This close association between physical health and mental health is a pervasive finding in research.

Regulating Gene Expression

With some of the same colleagues, I began a randomized controlled trial examining changes in gene expression in veterans after 10 EFT sessions (Church, Yount, Rachlin, Fox, & Nelms, 2015). Again, the study was difficult to fund and accomplish, and took many years to complete. But the results were worthwhile, and echoed the physical effects we'd identified in the cortisol study. We found that genes associated with inflammation in the body were downregulated, like turning down the dimmer switch on a lamp. Genes associated with immunity were upregulated, or turned up. The psychological symptoms of PTSD dropped by over 50%, echoing the results of earlier studies (Church, Hawk, et al., 2013; Geronilla, McWilliams, & Clond, 2014). This study shows that EFT is an epigenetic intervention, affecting the body at the most basic level of molecular biology, the DNA.

Many studies have now linked emotional nurturing to gene expression. Stress-regulation genes are turned on in the brains of newborn rats that are attentively licked and groomed by their mothers (Bagot, et al., 2012). When the brains of schizophrenics who have committed suicide are compared with the brains of mentally healthy people who died in accidents, the genes responsible for regulating stress are found to be turned off. The DNA is still there, but it's been inactivated by the stressful experiences of early childhood (Poulter et al., 2008; McGowan et al., 2008).

The link between physical and emotional symptoms has been understood for over a century. In his book *The Traumatic Neuroses of War,* psychiatrist Abram Kardiner (1941) described his observations of WWI veterans. Even people who had been highly functional before the war became detached (dissociated) and hypervigilant. He understood that PTSD is a condition of the body as much as the mind, writing that the "nucleus," or center of traumatic stress was a "physioneurosis" that took root in the body. Though science in Kardiner's time knew nothing of gene regulation, the physical basis of PTSD was observed by him and many other clinical professionals treating veterans and other traumatized populations.

Eye Movements Link Brain and Body

Another compelling link between brain and body was discovered after WWII. A British ophthalmologist published a book in which he noted that veterans had erratic eye movements (Traquair, 1944). A study confirming the link between eye movements and PTSD involved a collaboration between a psychiatrist and an ophthalmologist checking refs (Tym, Beaumont, & Lioulios, 2009). They studied 100 patients, and found that those with PTSD had persistent difficulty maintaining the stability of their peripheral vision while contemplating a traumatic event. After successful psychiatric treatment, however, the eye fluttering disappeared, and they were able to recall the event without either emotional distress or visual impairment. According to another published report, 90% of psychiatric patients have these visual anomalies (Tym, Dyck, & McGrath, 2000).

Neuroscientists don't know exactly why this association between traumatic memories and eye movements occurs. It may be linked to the ability of the brain to process a disturbing event. The limbic system contains structures that are responsible for turning short-term memories into long-term ones. This memory processing function is impaired in patients suffering from PTSD. This theory is discussed in an article in Scientific American (Rodriguez, 2012). It summarizes how research into EMDR, a therapy that is as effective as EFT for PTSD (Karatzias et al., 2011), demonstrates that the eye movements are an active ingredient of the therapy and not an inert placebo (Shapiro, 1989).

EFT uses a protocol for eye movements called the 9 Gamut Procedure (Callahan, 1985). It involves 9 actions performed while tapping a point called the "Gamut" point located on the Triple Warmer acupuncture meridian on the back of the hand. It includes eye movements, tapping, humming, and counting. The client moves his or her eyes slowly around a big circle at the extreme periphery of vision. The 9 Gamut Procedure is believed to engage parts of the brain involved in the nonverbal resolution of trauma. Other Clinical EFT Techniques such as the Floor to Ceiling Eye Roll (Feldenkrais, 1984) also use eye movements to reduce emotional distress. The developers of neuro-linguistic programming (NLP) believed that lateral eye movements correlate with aspects of experience such as internal dialog, kinesthetic sensations, and imagery (Bandler & Grinder, 1979). States such as REM sleep when the dreaming brain is in theta mode demonstrate that eye movements are part of the way the brain processes information.

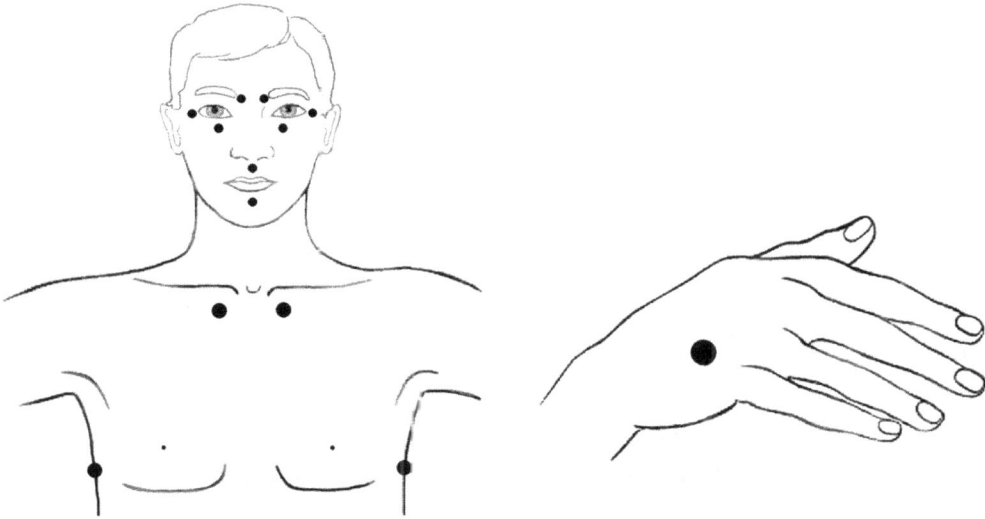

Figure 31. The acupressure points used in EFT.

The University of South Florida (USF) conducted a study of people with PTSD and depression, using a novel psychotherapeutic method called ART or Accelerated Resolution Therapy (Kip et al., 2012). ART uses eye movements, and has a client perform these while thinking about an emotionally triggering event. Researchers using ART found that the emotional charge held in such memories of traumatic events was rapidly reduced by eye movements. ART concludes by having clients pair the eye movements with the imagination of a desired outcome. According to the descriptions of the study, "the patient fluctuates between talking about a traumatic scene, and using the eye movements to help process that information to integrate the memories from traumatic events. The two major components of ART include minimizing or eliminating physiological response associated traumatic memories, and re-envisioning painful or disturbing experiences…" (Kip et al., 2012). Participants in the study experienced dramatic drops in both PTSD and depression symptoms, as well as improved sleep.

I use the 9 Gamut Procedure often during live coaching calls. While most EFT techniques focus on neutralizing particular traumatizing events, the 9 Gamut Procedure is effective at neutralizing a whole class of events simultaneously. If I'm working with a man whose father beat him often as a child, I'll use this technique on all the beatings instead of focusing on a particular beating. If I'm working with a woman who was sexually molested as a child, I'll use the 9 Gamut on the group of adverse experiences rather than identifying particular events. Usually, the SUD score of such clients for the entire class of events drops slowly over the course of half an hour. This approach is much more efficient than working on the events one by one. Once you're finished with the 9 Gamut, you can test the effect of your work by having the client focus on a single event and determining whether it's been neutralized.

When I'm working with clients in workshops, I watch their eyes closely. The erratic peripheral vision movements noted by Traquair are readily observable by the coach (though not by the client). Frequently, clients will move their eyes through every quadrant of the visual field except for one. They will consistently skip the same quadrant, like the hands of a clock going smoothly all the way around the face, but skipping between 3 and 6 o'clock. Once EFT has decreased the degree of distress, they no longer skip that quadrant, and their eye movements are smooth all the way around the field of peripheral vision. Following are a couple of case histories from the archives at EFT Universe.

Excessive Emotionality in a Brain-Damaged Child
by Tana Clark

I am an EFT practitioner and have a daughter who is brain damaged from birth. She did not get enough oxygen due to the cord around her neck for a lengthy time. I work with her almost on a daily basis with EFT. She can become very emotional at times, and it seems to take her hours to get over it. I have tapped with her on many occasions for this problem. I noticed that if I did not do the Gamut point, she didn't seem to settle down.

Finally, I just started doing the Gamut point when she "got stuck in the right brain." Now when she gets stuck, we immediately do a sequence and the 9 Gamut Procedure, and have 100% success rate to evaporate her emotion. When people get extremely emotional and can't seem to find a way out, they are stuck in the right brain.

Many people have problems being stuck in the right brain, and many of us have had the experience where we just can't stop crying. Doing the eye movements keeps our brain moving from right brain to left brain to right brain. It helps the brain to work together instead of being stuck on one side.

I also used it for a teenager whose family was moving; she was very upset about it and kept crying and crying. No amount of the other parts of EFT helped her feel less emotional. We moved to the 9 Gamut Procedure and, like magic, the tears dried up.

Using the short form of EFT, we often leave out the 9 Gamut Procedure. But if there is a large amount of emotion, it is extremely helpful. I couldn't do without it.

* * *

Resolution of Vertigo and a Car Crash Memory
by Edward Miner

I am a hypnotherapist and am always looking for better ways to help people get over their problems. Last evening, I talked with my sister, who lives in another state, about a condition of severe vertigo. She was in a minor automobile accident 2 weeks ago, experienced whiplash, and several days later started experiencing the vertigo.

I just got off the phone with her and want to report that she was symptom free when I hung up. In all, it took about 15 minutes to explain EFT and run through it about four times, testing between each run. I initially started the Setup with "Even though I have this vertigo and dizziness, I completely love and accept myself," but didn't see much movement. I adjusted to "Even though I have this vertigo and dizziness, I completely forgive myself or anyone else who may have contributed to it."

After a runthrough and a 9 Gamut Procedure, she was experiencing no symptoms. I had her move around a lot more and she found that when she tipped her head back she still had a dizzy feeling, but the rotation was slower. When I asked her if the feeling had an emotion, she said "annoyance," so we tapped on "the annoyance emotion." Subsequent SUD testing could find no more feelings of dizziness. She was amazed because she said that this was the worst time of day, just before she went to bed, and just prior to taking her medicine.

※ ※ ※

Clinical experience by thousands of EFT practitioners working with tens of thousands of clients has shown the 9 Gamut Procedure to be effective even when the other parts of EFT's Basic Recipe are unable to provide resolution to a problem. The cases offered above are typical. While the cognitive parts of EFT may reach the reasoning brain operating in an alpha-beta mode, it's likely that the 9 Gamut technique is reaching the nonverbal and preverbal parts of the brain. These are operating in that theta-delta superlearning trance. Clients receiving a long and thorough session with eye movements appear to go into a trance state. The practitioner then introduces Reminder Phrases from the traumatic memory. While these might produce high emotion before treatment, these triggers are removed by the 9 Gamut. The client still has the memory, but it no longer evokes strong emotion. In this way the 9 Gamut is able to treat memory tracks laid down in a preverbal state early in childhood, as well as those produced by severely traumatic adult experiences.

Memory Reconsolidation and Extinction

Until the early 2000s, the prevailing view in neuroscience was that, once an experience had been installed in long-term memory, it was difficult or impossible to change (Ecker, Ticic, & Hulley, 2012). Beliefs about the self and the world formed in early childhood through strong negative emotional associations were "locked into the brain by extraordinary durable synapses" (Ecker et al., p 3). They were believed to persist throughout the person's entire life. These memories were said to be "consolidated" into the neural network.

Then a series of studies with animals showed that, under certain conditions, even long-consolidated memories might become "labile," or malleable, and susceptible to change. This led to the discovery that "a consolidated memory can return...to a labile, sensitive state—in which it can be modified, strengthened, changed or even erased!" (Nader, 2003, p. 65). An ingenious set of experiments

Consolidation

STM
Short-term memory
Active state
AS

Reconsolidation

LTM
Long-term memory
Inactive state
AIS

Reactivation

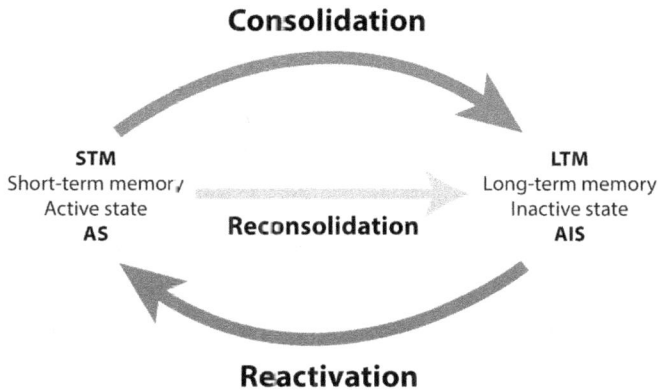

Figure 32. Memory reconsolidation.

applied the experience gained in animal studies to human trials (Schiller, Raio, & Phelps, 2012). It was able to measure the "reconsolidation window," the period of time after the arousal of a memory during which the memory was labile or open to revision. It found that window to be about six hours long. After the window had closed, the memory could no longer be revised. But if a revision occurred during the window, the effects held even a year later.

During the window, a traumatic memory, when combined with cues of safety from the present, may be reconsolidated as a non-threatening stimulus. When later remembered, the client no longer exhibits the fight-flight or freeze response. Clinicians began to ask if this model might be applied to psychology, allowing, for instance, PTSD patients to undo the strongly conditioned and consolidated memories that had traumatized them so deeply.

Certain treatment sequences seem to allow the brain to revise even long-consolidated beliefs. These protocols have now been precisely delineated. Ecker, Ticic, & Hulley (2012) call this the "transformation sequence," and break it into three interrelated stages:

1. Vivid re-exposure to the memory or experience must occur.

2. At the same time, a contradictory experience or memory ("juxtaposition experience") must be activated.

3. Several repetitions of the juxtaposition experience may be necessary in order for the new worldview to overwrite the old one.

Whether or not a therapist is aware of these three steps, Ecker and colleagues (2012) believe they are present in every successful therapeutic encounter. For this reason, Ecker calls this model a "meta-conceptualization" that applies to any type of therapy, not just to one school or technique.

Death in Vietnam: Joe's Story

A striking example of memory reconsolidation comes from "Joe," a disabled veteran with PTSD and multiple physical symptoms. During one of the six free sessions he received from his EFT practitioner after enrolling in the Veteran's Stress Project, Joe shared one of his most disturbing intrusive memories. His best friend, Ted, had been killed by a sniper in Vietnam. Ted and Joe used to go on patrol each day. Joe usually walked on the right, while Ted walked on the left. The day Ted was shot, they happened to have reversed positions, with Joe on the left. For over 40 years, Joe had suffered from "survivor's guilt," and his narrative about the event was "The bullet was meant for me."

After tapping as he described each component of the memory, Joe had a sudden cognitive shift, saying, "I'm realizing that, like I would have died for him, Ted would have died for me. He would have wanted to take the bullet for me, just like I thought I should have taken the bullet for him." This new narrative led Joe to feel a sense of resolution around the event, and he was no longer troubled by it. His SUD score went to zero. Though tapping was first used therapeutically decades before modern models of memory reconsolidation were developed, the components of EFT fit perfectly with the new model (Feinstein, 2015).

How EFT Applies the Three-Step Formula

In Step 1 of the formula identified by Ecker and colleagues (2012), Joe vividly recalled all the details of that day. EFT uses a Setup Statement to focus the client on the traumatic event, and a Reminder Phrase to keep attention on the event. Not only is the whole event recalled; Clinical EFT practitioners are trained to focus the client on all the details of the event, as well as sensory input that might be encoded in the trauma capsule. They might ask the client, "What did you see… taste… feel… touch… smell." An expert practitioner will mine the details of the event for every channel in which trauma might be encoded.

In EFT these are called "aspects" of a traumatizing event (Church, 2013). Research has shown that such concrete thinking is more likely to result in healing than abstract thinking (White & Wild, 2016). The principal investigator in this study, Dr Rachel White explained that, "Concrete processing is focusing on how a situation is unfolding, what is being experienced and what the next steps are. It differs from abstract processing, which is concerned with analyzing why something is happening, its implications, and asking 'what if' questions with no obvious answer." In EFT sessions, the practitioner keeps the client focused on the sensory aspects of the experience until the SUD level is zero.

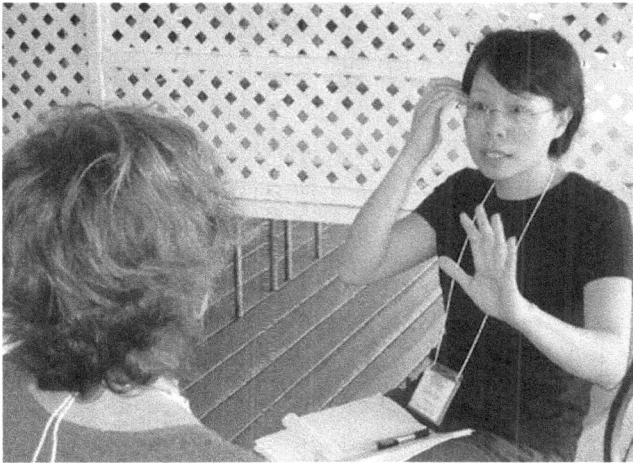

Figure 33. EFT session.

In Step 2, a contradictory experience is introduced in the form of tapping on acupoints. The soothing experience of tapping is juxtaposed with the upsetting memory being vividly recalled. The 9 Gamut Procedure may be added to the protocol. Limbic deactivation is occurring, PTSD-linked genes are being downregulated, and cortisol is being lowered, at the same time that the traumatic event is being held in memory.

In Step 3, repetition, the client taps repeatedly till the SUD score is reduced. This may take more than one round of EFT tapping. If the SUD level is not down to 0 after the first round, repeated rounds are performed. The 9 Gamut may be performed until the client's eyes are able to move smoothly through every degree of the peripheral visual field. The practitioner may dig for further details, and often clients access memory fragments they had forgotten or dissociated from before. An experienced Clinical EFT practitioner will keep asking questions until it is apparent that all the details and manifestations of the trauma have been extinguished.

At that point, the practitioner might instruct the client to make the details even more vivid or dramatic, in an effort to determine if the emotional charge of the memory has truly been extinguished. Once the client reports a SUD score of 0 for even the most troubling aspects of the memory, and can later recall the memory while remaining at a 0 SUD level, the work of memory reconsolidation and extinction is done.

These memories are not "extinguished" in the sense of being erased. What is extinguished is the emotional distress associated with the memory. This can be tested days, weeks, or months after the event by asking the client to remember the event again. The memory is usually still intact but without the emotional charge. The client may evidence a cognitive shift with statements like "It was awful, but I grew stronger through the experience" or "My dad was abused by his dad much worse than he abused me." Cognitive shifts might take the form of changes in visual perspective. The person might now perceive themselves as witnessing the event rather than being part of the scene. The event may come into sharp focus. Or the opposite may happen, with a previously clear image now becoming blurry.

In the 1920s Ivan Pavlov performed the basic experiments with dogs that demonstrated the phenomenon of conditioning, the process of developing a learned response to a stimulus. What is less well-known is that Pavlov's dogs lived in his Moscow basement, and were traumatized by a flood in 1924. Afterward, they had the equivalent of human PTSD, they had lost what Pavlov called their "instinct of purpose." He developed an "orienting response" to help them reorient themselves to the present in which the danger had passed, the Russian words for "what, what, where." These behavioral changes correlate with changes in the brain and endocrine system (Arden, 2012).

People with PTSD can also be reoriented away from the frozen state. A technique called "orienting EFT" directs clients to present-day cues while they think about trauma and tap on their acupressure points (Frank, 2016). The memory is then reconsolidated minus the emotional tags that produced the fight-flight or freeze response.

In this way, EFT is a short and efficient therapy for producing memory reconsolidation and the extinction of emotional cues, even in extreme trauma cases such as those resulting from the earthquake in Haiti and the genocide in Rwanda, and long-standing PTSD such as that found in Vietnam veterans. Feinstein (2010), reviewing eight studies examining the effect of acupoint tapping on PTSD, maintains that: "(a) tapping on selected acupoints (b) during imaginal exposure (c) quickly and permanently reduces maladaptive fear responses to traumatic memories and related cues."

The following detailed account by EFT practitioner Sophia Cayer illustrates the process of identifying and releasing layers of trauma. EFT is able to defuse the intense emotions generated by the veteran's memories, and transform core issues.

Layers of Trauma
by Sophia Cayer

John is a Gulf War veteran in his late 30s, married, with small children. He managed to cope with the side effects of his war experience fairly well until the

September 11 event in New York City, which threw him into full-blown PTSD. At that point, everything began falling apart.

Situations such as this are far more common than most realize. Delayed reactions are important considerations for anyone working with veterans and their families. Many times, veterans arrive home and initially exhibit minimal or no side effects resulting from their war experiences. Others manage to successfully mask or ignore related emotions. They put up a valiant front, doing their best to resume life as they used to know it. Therefore family and friends think everything is almost back to normal.

Then without warning and for seemingly no reason, things start falling apart. As time goes by, even subtle events can spark flashbacks that trigger PTSD symptoms. I have seen veterans triggered while driving because the tire treads on a truck in front of them reminded them of the tires on military vehicles. Video games and newsreels are things they quickly learn to avoid.

Major events such as 9/11 or any event they perceive as a threat can trigger flashbacks, intense emotions, physical symptoms, a constant sense of hypervigilance, anxiety, sudden unexplainable bursts of anger, nightmares, insomnia, and other PTSD symptoms. Friends and family members can be equally traumatized, as they don't understand what is happening. They, too, need care.

John had been prescribed every available medication believed to help with PTSD symptoms, to no avail. He and his wife had flown all over the country trying various treatments in their search for answers. Less than 2 months before I met with him, John completed an 8-week PTSD treatment program offered by the V.A. He told me that being among his comrades in itself had offered comfort and he felt a little better while he was at the facility. The instant he went home and back into "the real world," however, his challenges returned. Even with all the medications, he was depressed and lethargic. He spent most of his day slumped in a recliner and couldn't find the motivation to attempt the mental or physical exercises that had been suggested to help his condition. He was exploding at the drop of the hat and found himself constantly arguing with his wife and children.

John was consumed by sadness as well as fear and anger, and he told me that the only reason suicide wasn't an option was that he was too concerned about the pain it would cause his family. He was guilt-ridden about the state of affairs with his family and felt like a failure when it came to military service.

I always make it a point to inquire about the level of anxiety the person feels about even attempting EFT. Most of the time, it is a last-ditch effort after a number of disappointing avenues have been explored. Most veterans are not only anxious, they are also frightened and uneasy. I tap first on whatever they are feeling, whatever misgivings are there before we go any further. In my experience, this approach opens the door to achieving more profound results in a shorter period of time. It is also a great way to demonstrate how quickly the technique can help them achieve results, which also helps gain their trust and confidence.

When I asked John how he felt about doing this work, he said he was worried, didn't know what to expect, and was disappointed that his wife couldn't be there with him. "She's been here with me most of the time," he said, and I could see emotions and tears beginning to well up.

He said the worst part was not knowing what to expect. His discomfort level was already at an 8 and he was feeling it in his stomach. He described it as a knot, a tightening up, or tension.

As he was brand new to EFT, I said, "Let me show you how silly it is. Let's just take a crack at it and see how it lands for you and how quickly it can work. If it begins to feel too intense, just let me know. You don't have to tell anything, just focus on the tightening up."

KC (Karate Chop): *Even though I have this anxiety in my stomach, I love and respect myself.*

He couldn't say the words "I love and respect myself" and broke into tears. I assured him he didn't have to say the words and that together we would get through it.

We began again with different words:

KC (Karate Chop): *Even though I have all this anxiety in my stomach, I choose peace.*

TH (Top of Head): *All this anxiety.*

EB (Eyebrow): *All this anxiety.*

SE (Side of Eye): *All this anxiety.*

UE (Under Eye): *It is sitting in my stomach.*

UN (Under Nose): *I don't know what to expect.*

Ch (Chin): *I have been through enough.*

CB (Collarbone): *I just want to feel better.*

UA (Under the Arm): *All this anxiety.*

TH (Top of Head): *All this fear and anti-cipation.*

EB (Eye Brow): *I choose peace.*

SE (Side of Eye): *This anxiety.*

UE (Under Eye): *All this tension in my stomach.*

UN (Under Nose): *This anxiety in my stomach.*

Ch (Chin): *I choose peace.*

Sensing a major change in his demeanor and voice, I asked him to relax, breathe, and let me know how his stomach was feeling.

He seemed a little surprised when he announced, "Better—I am probably at a 3 or 4. That's pretty neat!"

I encouraged him by reminding him that with this wonderful self-empowerment tool, he could soon feel comfortable working on his own, dealing with things as they came up. I also reminded him that he could tap preemptively. The realization that he could be in charge and in control of his emotions as he worked through issues on his own was an empowering thought, one that encouraged the healing process.

KC: *Even though I still have some of this anticipation in my stomach, I choose peace.*

Even though I still have some anticipation in my stomach, and I am not sure what to expect, I choose peace anyway.

TH: *This remaining tightness in my stomach.*

EB: *This remaining tightness.*

SE: *This anticipation in my stomach.*

UE: *I don't know what to expect.*

UN: *This anticipation.*

Ch: *Something else to try.*

CB: *I don't know what to expect.*

UA: *But I choose peace anyway.*

TH: *This anticipation.*

EB: *I choose to feel better.*

SE: *I choose to let go of all this anticipation.*

UE: *And to have peace within.*

At this point, he reported his stomach felt better and he felt he was probably down to 1 or 0. "Just a tiny little bit" remained.

TH: *This tiny little bit.*

EB: *That is still sitting in my stomach.*

SE: *I choose peace.*

UE: *I choose peace.*

UN: *This tiny little bit.*

Ch: *Still sitting in my stomach.*

CB: *I choose to believe in me.*

Now the stomach tightness was gone and he felt ready to proceed. As we continued to work on the more intense and complex issues together, he began to see how EFT might help him get through the days more easily.

It is important to encourage persistence when people will be working on their own, so that they realize there is no need to feel discouraged if they happen to experience intensities going up and down or find themselves switching from one aspect of the problem to another.

Now that John was feeling more relaxed and comfortable, knowing what to expect, it was time to move forward.

Based on John's vacant expression when he arrived, which is typical of those severely affected by PTSD, and his rapid shifts from no apparent emotion to high emotion, I knew it was particularly important to be mindful and cautious as we moved forward. I realized that he could experience difficulty in getting to core issues because they were blocked, or he could find that some memories were easily triggered. These are important considerations if you are new to dealing with PTSD.

When I inquired as to what he felt was his most pressing issue, he said it was his depression and anger, but he could offer little else. With a little gentle probing on my part, he recalled that the onset occurred in 2000 or 2001, but he still couldn't connect it with anything specific.

Knowing there had been issues with being in and out of the service, I asked John where things stood with his military career. He told me that he wasn't connected any longer with the military. He had left in 1998, and the doctors believed that his PTSD was set off by the events of September 11, 2001. He attempted to reenter the military following 9/11 and was denied due to his physical condition.

I could hear the emotion in his voice, so I immediately interrupted to ask what he was feeling as he relayed the story. His one-word answer was "Anger."

In an attempt to be more specific, I asked, "Anger with the government or anger about them not letting you reenlist?"

John replied, "Both. Anger at 9/11 and anger that I couldn't do anything about it."

I could feel and sense a lot more than anger and quickly received John's confirmation of deep sadness. We tapped for:

KC: *Even though I am filled with all this anger and sadness—there was nothing I could do, they wouldn't even let me try—I am okay anyway.*

Even though I am filled with all this sadness and anger—I wanted to help and there was nothing I could do—I choose peace anyway.

TH: *All this anger and sadness.*

EB: *I am absolutely furious.*

SE: *They wouldn't let me help.*

UE: *They wouldn't let me help.*

UN: *All this grief and sadness.*

Ch: *I am absolutely furious!*

CB: *Why did this have to happen?*

UA: *It just wasn't right.*

TH: *I am angry with the government.*

EB: *They stopped me.*

SE: *I am really furious.*

UE: *I wanted to help.*

UN: *And they wouldn't let me.*

Ch: *They told me no.*

CB: *All this anger and sadness.*

UA: *All this grief and sadness.*

TH: *This grief and sadness.*

We had taken the edge off, but it was obvious that related issues and aspects were bubbling up. Since he was having difficulty voicing anything, I asked, "Did you lose someone close to you in 9/11?"

John said, "No, but I dealt with a lot of dead in the first Gulf war." I could feel myriad emotions emanating and knew his mind was racing from event to event and feeling to feeling. We managed to determine that the most predominant feelings were related to rejection by the military.

To help find a core issue, an important underlying event or memory that would bring John's attention from the vague and general to the specific and detailed, I began asking questions related to when and how he learned that he could not rejoin the military. Was it over the phone, in person, or in a letter?

"It was done by computer," he said. "They opened a site taking back prior enlisted. I filled out the paperwork and got rejected. They told me I had too many problems and wasn't medically able, even though I did 8 and a half years with a screwed-up back that got injured in service."

When I asked, "Does that make you angry?" his voice rose through a swell of emotion and tears until he was almost screaming, "I'm not really angry at the government—I love my government. I would fight and die for my country. I don't know who I am angry at."

I said, "It doesn't matter. You don't have to know." It was impossible and unnecessary to attempt to sort anything out, so we simply began tapping:

KC: *Even though I am angry and sad at the same time and I am not even sure what this is all about, I am okay.*

Even though I am angry and sad that they rejected me, I am okay.

TH: *That news that came through the computer.*

EB: *They rejected me.*

SE: *I really wanted to go.*

UE: *I wanted to do my duty.*

UN: *I wanted to be there.*

Ch: *They told me no.*

CB: *All these emotions.*

UA: *All this anger and sadness.*

TH: *They told me no.*

EB: *They wouldn't take me even after all I had done.*

SE: *They wouldn't take me.*

UE: *All this rejection.*

UN: *All this sadness and anger that I really don't understand.*

Ch: *This sadness and anger.*

CB: *They said no.*

UA: *This sadness and anger.*

TH: *I saw it in the computer.*

EB: *They said no.*

SE: *All this anger and sadness.*

UE: *This deep anger and sadness.*

UN: *All this frustration.*

CB: *Deep sadness and anger.*

UA: *All this deep sadness.*

John felt the intensity had dropped from a 10 to a 5. It is important to note that many major shifts in intensity are quite common in this situation. Frequently, this happens because it is impossible for PTSD victims to remain focused on one aspect of an issue, or even one issue.

I asked, "Which feels more intense, the anger or the sadness?" He replied, "Both feel about the same."

He now felt he might be able to remain focused on receiving the news. Disappointment and despair were intensifying.

KC: *Even though I'm still at a 5, I've still got this anger and disappointment and all this deep sadness, I choose peace.*

Even though I have all this deep sadness and all this anger because they said no, I am okay anyway. I choose peace.

Even though I have all this deep sadness and all this anger because they said no, I am okay anyway. I choose peace.

TH: *All this remaining anger and sadness.*

EB: *This feeling of despair.*

SE: *They wouldn't take me back.*

UE: *All this anger and despair.*

UN: *This deep sadness.*

Ch: *I couldn't believe that news.*

CB: *I didn't want to hear that news.*

UA: *All this anger and sadness.*

TH: *I am still carrying it.*

EB: *This anger and sadness.*

SE: *They said no.*

UN: *This remaining anger and sadness.*

Ch: *Remaining anger and sadness.*

I stopped at this point because I could sense a marked improvement. John reported feeling relaxed and "I'd say I am at a 0." It was time to test. I asked him to picture himself in front of the computer getting the news and see how it felt.

John said he could see himself there with his brother. As he began to tell me about reading it on the screen, I could sense his emotions on the rise.

I asked, "What does it feel like now?" He replied, "It is just the rejection that hurts." He felt it was at a 3 or 4, and he was feeling it in his chest and stomach.

KC: *Even though I still have this sense of rejection in my chest and stomach, I choose peace. I choose to believe in me.*

Even though I feel this rejection in my chest and stomach, I choose peace, I choose to believe in me.

TH: *This rejection.*

EB: *I couldn't believe that letter.*

SE: *That terrible letter.*

UE: *That rejection.*

UN: *Those rejection words.*

Ch: *It still hurts.*

CB: *It still hurts.*

UA: *All that rejection.*

IW: *All that rejection.*

OW: *They rejected me.*

9G: *They rejected me.*

IW: *All this rejection.*

OW: *I choose to believe in me.*

In this tapping sequence, I included two optional tapping points, the Inside Wrist (IW) and Outside Wrist (OW), plus the 9 Gamut Procedure (9G).

John returned to the computer screen in his mind's eye to read his rejection letter again. This time he reported it was just another screen. He was quite pleased that EFT was working and said that now he had "calmed down big time."

He felt better equipped to begin dealing with some of the traumatic events, so we attempted to gently approach the most haunting ones. It is important to remember that, even when someone begins to experience relief, his or her enthusiasm may lead both of you to believe it is time to forge full speed ahead. Please continue to approach things in a gentle and subtle manner. That euphoria and the return of the "I can handle it!" feeling may prove to be short lived and, in a matter of minutes, other events will evoke new rivers of emotion.

Though it is best if you can "sneak up" on events, these events may continually replay in the person's mind. John reported that many of the scenes came to him like a movie screen that started in the morning and ran all day long. "If something happens in the house," he said, "I explode for no reason at all. I am already fired up. They've got me on all of this crap [medications] that's supposed to help, but nothing works."

I reminded him that he had a new "secret weapon" and that it was possible for him to have more than temporary relief.

At this point, I thought we would set to work on the nonstop movies. Well, that's not the way it went. We started down that path, but as we worked, it led us in different directions. Remember that these are complex cases and it is important to follow and not lead, letting the person work through events and memories as they present themselves. The following will clearly demonstrate how winding the trail can become and how essential it is to let things unfold on their own.

Out of concern about triggering those reading this book, I offer limited details, but the general drift of the tuning-into-events conversation started when John said, " I dealt with something in the Gulf War. It was the scariest thing I ever did in my life, something we never practiced before."

Again, myriad emotions were before us, but the most intense was his sense of guilt, the feeling that he had failed to complete his mission according to the rules.

KC: *Even though I am feeling guilty — I feel like a failure as a _____.*

He couldn't say the words, and tears and emotions intensified. Realizing that "failure" was the trigger and knowing he was more than tuned in, I eliminated the word. No need to traumatize further in order for EFT to get the job done.

Even though I am filled with guilt, I am okay.

TH: *All this guilt, all this guilt.*

EB: *I still see that image.*

SE: *I should have _____.*

UE: *All this guilt, all this guilt.*

UN: *I can't let it go…why didn't I _____?*

Ch: *All this guilt, all this guilt.*

CB: *All this guilt — why didn't I _____?*

UA: *I should have _____.*

TH: *All this guilt.*

EB: *All this guilt.*

SE: *This guilt.*

John said he felt better, so we did a little probing to see how intense the pictures were, as well as his feeling of guilt. That brief tapping brought him down to a 3.

KC: *Even though I have this remaining guilt, I choose peace.*

Even though I have this remaining guilt, I choose peace.

TH: *Remaining guilt.*

EB: *I should have _____.*

SE: *I can't forgive myself.*

UE: *All this guilt.*

UN: *Remaining guilt.*

Ch: *Remaining guilt.*

CB: *All this remaining guilt.*

I felt a shift and when I checked in with John, he reported feeling "neutral" about an event he had been carrying since 1991, or for 17 years.

He was a little stunned that this could really be the case, but he was beginning to be impressed with his EFT experience. He then shared with me that, normally, after being triggered to the extent he was as we talked and worked together, his anger would have remained with him for hours.

He told me that my using the word "failure" was very triggering, even though I was using his words. I asked how true that still felt and why it still seemed to feel true.

He told me that he had been involved since elementary school in some form of military association. In one way or another, the military had always been part of his identity. He was convinced that getting out of the service was a big mistake, and he simply couldn't put it behind him.

As we talked, it became apparent that he was afraid he would lose memories he treasured because, to him, the service was family during the times in his life when he had no family. This is something to consider when you are working with those new to EFT. They need to understand that EFT is not going to erase positive memories.

I assured him that he could put the bad behind him without losing the positive. "This isn't going to make you forget, but it will help you neutralize the emotions. Events will be things that happened, but they won't continue to steal your life from you."

He said, "That's what they are doing — stealing my whole life."

Emotions were rapidly rising as he spoke about almost losing his wife because of arguments. In the moment, he was caught up in what he saw as his big mistake, leaving the service:

KC: *Even though it was all a big mistake I can't take back, I choose peace anyway. Even though there was too much going on and I didn't know how to handle it, I did the best I knew how — but I want to be happy with the way things turned out — I forgive myself. There is just too much. It is all too painful.*

TH: *How could I ever let this go?*

EB: *It is too painful. It is too big.*

SE: *But maybe if I take it one piece at a time.*

UE: *I can create peace for myself.*

UN: *Even though I feel like my past has stolen the present.*

Ch: *I choose to be in the present.*

UA: *It is too much, it is too big, I can't change it.*

TH: *Or maybe I can.*

EB: *Maybe I can embrace the present and enjoy the now.*

SE: *Letting go of all this deep sadness.*

UE: *Letting go of all this pain from the past.*

UN: *Letting go and choosing peace*

Ch: *Letting go.*

CB: *Choosing the present.*

John's intensity was greatly reduced, but I knew we had a ways to go. In an effort to reassess, I asked him to repeat a statement about his sense of feeling lost now that he was no longer in the service. He simply couldn't do it and broke into tears, as he said, "I hate not being there."

Even though I hate not being there, it was my life, I feel lost without it, I choose peace. Even though I hate not being there—it was my life for so many years—I love and forgive myself. I choose peace.

TH: *It was my life, from the time I was 7—it was like my family.*

EB: *It was all I could really count on.*

SE: *I miss it.*

UE: *It was all I knew.*

UN: *From the time I was 7.*

Ch: *I miss it.*

CB: *I'm lost without it.*

UA: *I am angry and filled with despair.*

IW: *I miss it.*

OW: *I am lost without it.*

TH: *Nothing feels the same.*

The emotional ups and downs were constant, making it apparent that he was roaming through various issues and aspects. So we took a breather for a moment and I attempted to hone in on a more specific and intense aspect.

Many family circumstances had made John feel that he needed to leave the service. Thirty days later, however, he found himself filled with regret and headed to a recruitment office for reenlistment. They would take him back, but he would lose rank and end up taking a pay cut. He would be outranked by the very soldiers he had been in charge of a month earlier. He couldn't bring himself to accept it, so he walked away. There was anger about the fact that they wouldn't check his records to see that he had already given them many years of service and had been due to pick up a new rank when he left.

As he shared this with me, however, additional aspects, issues, and events were making themselves known. I allowed him the opportunity to download, as in the middle of all this, he had shared with me that he was revealing things to me that he had never shared with anyone. And of course, it ended up bringing us to exactly where we needed to be, in the middle of an emotion-packed image from his daily movies.

KC: Even though I still have this incredibly vivid image, and it still has me feeling angry and guilty because I didn't perform the way I should have, I forgive myself. Even though I can't get this image out of my mind, it is incredibly vivid—still filled with guilt and anger. I should have done it differently—I forgive myself.

TH: *This image.*

EB: *This vivid image.*

SE: *I see it every day.*

UE: *See it all the time.*

UN: *It really bothers me.*

Ch: *I am angry with myself.*

CB: *Disappointed in me, I failed.*

UA: *I still see that image.*

TH: *Vivid image.*

EB: *That image.*

SE: *It's with me all the time.*

UE: *I see it every day.*

UN: *That image.*

Ch: *That vivid image.*

CB: *Still angry with myself.*

UA: *That image, I didn't do what they taught me to do.*

At this point, John was doing his best to stifle a yawn. I told him to just let it happen, knowing that he was processing the many changes he was experiencing.

IW: *Vivid image.*

OW: *That vivid image.*

9G: *Didn't do what they taught me to do.*

IW: *I keep flashing back there.*

OW: *That vivid image.*

9G: *I see it every day.*

TH: *I see it all the time.*

EB: *I see it now.*

SE: *That image.*

UE: *I am still angry with myself.*

UN: *Why didn't I do what they taught me to do?*

Ch: *I can't let this go.*

CB: *I won't let this go.*

UA: *It's my anger and you can't have it.*

TH: *It is serving me well.*

EB: *I can't let this go.*

SE: *I won't let this go.*

UE: *This vivid image.*

UN: *I can't forgive myself.*

Ch: *This image.*

CB: *This vivid image.*

UA: *All this anger with myself.*

TH: *All this anger with myself.*

John was feeling much better, so we did some testing. He reran the scene in his mind and then detailed the image, as best he could. There was no emotional charge and he shared with me that the image in his mind was now of his family, and his feeling was that of hope. In a matter of seconds, however, he said, "It doesn't feel bad—*for now.*" When I asked about "for now," an obvious tail-ender, he told me he was sure it would pop up again later and get him fired up.

Sure, it is possible that some remnants remain to be cleared, or that new aspects, including but not limited to smells or sounds, might surface. But I reminded him that if that were the case, with a little persistent tapping he could experience the same sense of relief and hope he had today.

Concerned about his doubts and the obvious tail-ender, we went to work. Here's a sample of the language.

KC: *Even though a part of me may think this is too good to be true, and those awful feelings are bound to come back—how could I be rid of it so easily? I am willing to trust and believe in me.*

TH: *I think I like feeling better.*

EB: *I might even be able to love and forgive my-self.*

SE: *This is too weird.*

UE: *How could this possibly be true after all these years?*

UN: *All these meds.*

Ch: *All those things I tried.*

CB: *Nothing's made a difference.*

UA: *How could it be so simple?*

TH: *Where were you when I needed you?*

EB: *Maybe I can believe in this.*

SE: *Even though it seems unbelievable.*

UE: *Too good to be true.*

UN: *I choose to be persistent.*

Ch: *Because I know I can overcome.*

We both knew that work remained to be done, but for the first time in years, he was hopeful. He asked, "Why aren't they using this stuff at the V.A.?"

That's a good question. I am working on it, but, in the meantime, we all need to be giving our all to spreading the word and getting EFT to as many as humanly possible, most especially to veterans and their families.

※ ※ ※

I included this detailed case history because it is a comprehensive example of the depth, complexity, and potential for healing that can occur when using EFT to help resolve PTSD. There are many more case histories and reports by veterans on the Stress Project web site and on EFT Universe. They represent the human faces behind the excellent results demonstrated in clinical trials of EFT for PTSD. Behind every number, there is a group of suffering human beings, and their stories along with the data present a multifaceted picture of the healing potential of energy therapies.

The Future of Psychology and Medicine

I believe we are entering a new era in psychology and medicine as dramatic as the elimination of most infectious diseases at the start of the 20th century. Research shows that body-based approaches such as EFT and EMDR have the ability to remediate most mental health conditions in just a few sessions. Treatment time frames range from one session for phobias (Wells, Polglase, Andrews, Carrington, & Baker, 2003) to 10 sessions for difficult diagnoses such as PTSD (Church, Yount, Rachlin, Fox, & Nelms, 2015).

Imagine these therapies being available as front-line medical care. Imagine every veteran having access to EFT, and international initiatives to offer EFT to large groups of traumatized people. Imagine a society as dedicated to eliminating these mental health problems as we were to eliminating infectious disease.

Imagine depression, anxiety, phobias and PTSD becoming as rare as polio, cholera, or typhoid fever. The infectious disease revolution was accomplished quickly, and the mental health revolution might occur just as quickly.

Figure 34. Group EFT session.

Imagine if future generations of children are raised by parents who have healed their own traumatic histories. Imagine if every child with test anxiety, social phobia, or public speaking anxiety had the tools of energy psychology at his or her fingertips. Imagine teams of mental health professionals treating survivors of natural and human-caused disasters, alleviating the suffering that would otherwise occur.

This is all very possible. As a society, we now have the tools to accomplish this, just as we accomplished the eradication of many infectious diseases generations ago. Having the tools, we now need the vision and the will to use them effectively. I believe that collectively we may well make this decision, resulting in a future society very different than the one we live in today. As we tap away our own individual traumatization, we will enjoy happier and more balanced lives. As we offer these methods to others, we contribute to a happier and more balanced society. Our children and grandchildren will thank us, just as we thank the heroes who gave us a world free of most of the diseases from which previous generations suffered. We are part of a large social movement that I believe will result in a future very much better than our past.

Summary

- An event is characterized as traumatic when: 1) the person perceives it as a threat to her or his physical survival; 2) it overwhelms the individual's coping capacity, producing a sense of powerlessness; 3) it produces a feeling of isolation and aloneness; and 4) it violates the person's expectations.

- Psychological trauma is not a merely psychological problem. High stress is linked to virtually every type of physical disease, and there is an undeniable link between unresolved childhood trauma and adult disease.

- Your body can't tell the difference between a stressful thought and a stressful event. Stressful thoughts send your body into the fight-or-flight response; thus you produce all the neurophysiology of stress in your body while having no objective reason to be on high alert.

- Stressed brains reinforce the neural pathways dedicated to carrying stress-related signals, at the expense of the brain regions responsible for memory, learning, and making high-quality executive decisions. PTSD symptoms often get worse over time, as neuroplasticity builds up the circuits of stress.

- Dissociation is a coping mechanism that compartmentalizes a traumatic event in a "trauma capsule," which allows the individual to keep functioning in an inescapable situation.

- Tapping while thinking of a stressful event signals that one is safe in the here and now, which breaks the association in the brain's limbic system between the stressful memory and the fight-or-flight response. It provides one with a base of security from which one can begin to unpack one's trauma capsules.

- Each veteran with PTSD costs an estimated $1.4 million to treat. The cumulative cost to society of treating the remaining 400,000 Vietnam veterans with PTSD and the estimated 500,000 PTSD-afflicted veterans of the recent Middle East wars exceeds $1 trillion. The cost of six sessions with an EFT practitioner for every one of these veterans comes to $300 million.

- In a study of cognitive behavioral therapy for PTSD, often the treatment of choice, half the participants did not respond to treatment, in contrast to EFT studies that show upward of 80% veterans permanently rehabilitated.

References

American Psychiatric Association. (1994). *Diagnostic and statistical manual of mental disorders* (4th ed.). Washington, DC: Author.

American Psychological Association. (2010). *Publication manual of the American psychological association* (6th Ed.). Washington: American Psychological Association.

Anderson, C. M., Teicher, M. H., Polcari, A., & Renshaw, P. F. (2002). Abnormal T2 relaxation time in the cerebellar vermis of adults sexually abused in childhood: potential role of the vermis in stress-enhanced risk for drug abuse. *Psychoneuroendocrinology, 27*(1), 231–244.

Angell, M. (2005). *The truth about the drug companies: How they deceive us and what to do about it.* New York, NY: Random House.

Arden, J. (2012). PTSD, neurodynamics, and memory. In Church, D., & Marohn, S. (Eds.) (2013). *The clinical EFT handbook: A definitive resource for practitioners, scholars, clinicians and researchers.* Santa Rosa, CA: Energy Psychology Press.

Bach, D., Groesbeck, G., Stapleton, P., Banton, S., Blickheuser, K., & Church, D. (2016). Clinical EFT (Emotional Freedom Techniques) improves multiple physiological markers of health. Presented at Omega Institute, October 15, 2016.

Bagot, R. C., Zhang, T. Y., Wen, X., Nguyen, T. T., Nguyen, H. B., Diorio, J., Wong, T. P., & Meaney, M. J. (2012). Variations in postnatal maternal care and the epigenetic regulation of metabotropic glutamate receptor 1 expression and hippocampal function in the rat. *Proceedings of the National Academy of Sciences USA, 109*(Suppl 2), 17200–17207. doi: 10.1073/pnas.1204599109.

Bandler, R., & Grinder, J. (1979). *Frogs into princes: Neuro linguistic programming.* Moab, UT: Real People.

Belanoff, J. K., Kalehzan, M., Sund, B., Ficek, S. K., & Schatzberg, A. F. (2001). Cortisol activity and cognitive changes in psychotic major depression. *American Journal of Psychiatry, 158*(10), 1612–1616.

Beck, R. (1986). Mood modification with ELF magnetic fields: A preliminary exploration. *Archaeus, 4*(48).

Boris, N. W., Fueyo, M., & Zeanah, C. H. (1997). The clinical assessment of attachment in children under five. *Journal of the American Academy of Child and Adolescent Psychiatry, 36*(2), 291–293.

Brodie, E. M. (2015). Dealing with trauma using the non-local mind and shamanic soul retrieval. *Energy Psychology: Theory, Research, and Treatment, 7*(2), 45–56. doi:10.9769/EPJ.2015.11.1.EB.

Callahan, R. (1985). Five minute phobia cure: Dr. Callahan's treatment for fears, phobias, and self-sabotage. Blair, NE: Enterprise.

Callahan, R. (2000). *Tapping the healer within: Using Thought Field Therapy to instantly conquer your fears, anxieties, and emotional distress.* New York, NY: McGraw-Hill.

Chambless, D., & Hollon, S. D. (1998). Defining empirically supported therapies. *Journal of Consulting and Clinical Psychology, 66*, 7–18.

Cherkin, D. C., Sherman, K. J., Avins, A. L., Erro, J. H., Ichikawa, L., Barlow, W. E.,... Deyo, R. A. (2009). A randomized trial comparing acupuncture, simulated acupuncture, and usual care for chronic low back pain. *Archives of Internal Medicine, 169*(9), 858–866. doi:10.1001/archinternmed.2009.65.

Church, D. (2012). The dark side of neural plasticity. *Energy Psychology: Theory, Research, and Treatment, 4*(2), 11–14.

Church, D. (2013). *The EFT manual* (3rd ed.). Santa Rosa, CA: Energy Psychology Press.

Church, D. (2014). Pain, depression, and anxiety after PTSD symptom remediation in veterans. *Explore: The Journal of Science and Healing, 10*(3), 162–169.

Church, D., & Brooks, A. J. (2014). CAM and energy psychology techniques remediate PTSD symptoms in veterans and spouses. *Explore: The Journal of Science and Healing, 10*(1), 24–33.

Church, D., Geronilla, L., & Dinter, I. (2009). Psychological symptom change in veterans after six sessions of EFT (Emotional Freedom Techniques): An observational study. *International Journal of Healing and Caring, 9*(1).

Church, D., Hawk, C., Brooks, A., Toukolehto, O., Wren, M., Dinter, I., & Stein, P. (2013). Psychological trauma symptom improvement in veterans using EFT (Emotional Freedom Techniques): A randomized controlled trial. *Journal of Nervous and Mental Disease, 201*, 153–160.

Church, D., Yount, G., & Brooks, A. J. (2012). The effect of Emotional Freedom Techniques (EFT) on stress biochemistry: A randomized controlled trial. *Journal of Nervous and Mental Disease, 200*, 891–896. doi:10.1097/NMD.0b013e31826b9fc1.

Church, D., Yount, G., Rachlin, K., Fox, L., & Nelms, J. (2015). Epigenetic effects of PTSD remediation in veterans using Clinical EFT (Emotional Freedom Techniques): A randomized controlled trial. Paper presented at the Association for Comprehensive Energy Psychology (ACEP) conference, Reston, VA, May 30, 2015. Submitted for publication.

Church, D., Stern, S., Boath, E., Stewart, A., Feinstein, D., & Clond, M. (2017). Using Emotional Freedom Techniques (EFT) to treat PTSD in veterans: A review of the evidence, survey of practitioners, and proposed clinical guidelines. *The Permanente Journal* (in press).

Craig, G., & Fowlie, A. (1995). *Emotional freedom techniques: The manual*. Sea Ranch, CA: Gary Craig.

Damasio, A. R., Grabowski, T. J., Bechara, A., Damasio, H., Ponto, L. L., Parvizi, J., & Hichwa, R. D. (2000). Subcortical and cortical brain activity during the feeling of self-generated emotions. *Nature Neuroscience, 3*(10), 1049–1056.

Darwin, C. (1872). *The expression of the emotions in man and animals*. New York, NY: Appleton.

Deacon, B. J., & Lickel, J. J. (2009). On the brain disease model of mental disorders. *Behavior Therapist, 32*(6), 113–118.

Ecker, B., Ticic, R., & Hulley, L. (2012). *Unlocking the emotional brain: Eliminating symptoms at their roots using memory reconsolidation*. New York, NY: Routledge.

Fang, J., Jin, Z., Wang, Y., Li, K., Kong, J., Nixon, E. E.,...Hui, K. K.-S. (2009). The salient characteristics of the central effects of acupuncture needling: Limbic-paralimbic-neocortical network modulation. *Human Brain Mapping, 30*, 1196–1206. doi:10.1002/hbm.20583.

Feinstein, D. (2010). Rapid treatment of PTSD: Why psychological exposure with acupoint tapping may be effective. *Psychotherapy: Theory, Research, Practice, Training, 47*, 385–402. doi:10.1037/a0021171.

Feinstein, D. (2015). How energy psychology changes deep emotional learnings. *Neuropsychotherapist, 10*, 39–49.

Feldenkrais, M. (1984). *The master moves.* Cupertino, CA: Meta Publications.

Felitti, V. J., Anda, R. F., Nordenberg, D., Williamson, D. F., Spitz, A. M., Edwards, V.,… Marks, J. S. (1998). Relationship of childhood abuse and household dysfunction to many of the leading causes of death in adults. The Adverse Childhood Experiences (ACE) Study. *American Journal of Preventive Medicine, 14*(4), 245–258.

Figley, C. R. (Ed.). (1986). *Trauma and its wake: Traumatic stress theory, research and intervention.* New York, NY: Brunner/Mazel.

Ford, D. E., & Erlinger, T. P. (2004). Depression and C-reactive protein in US adults: data from the Third National Health and Nutrition Examination Survey. *Archives of Internal Medicine, 164*(9), 1010–1014.

Frank, A. (2016). *How to want sex again: Rekindling passion with EFT.* Seattle, WA: Difference.

Freedman, A. M., Kaplan, H. I., & Sadock, B. J. (1975). *Comprehensive textbook of psychiatry.* New York, NY: Williams & Wilkins.

Frodl, T., Reinhold, E., Koutsouleris, N., Reiser, M., & Meisenzahl, E. M. (2010). Interaction of childhood stress with hippocampus and prefrontal cortex volume reduction in major depression. *Journal of Psychiatric Research, 44*(13), 799–807.

Geary, D. C., & Huffman, K. J. (2002). *Brain and cognitive evolution: forms of modularity and functions of mind. Psychological Bulletin, 128*(5) 667–698.

Geronilla, L., McWilliams, M., & Clond, M. (2014, April 17). EFT (Emotional Freedom Techniques) remediates PTSD and psychological symptoms in veterans: A randomized controlled replication trial. Presented at the Grand Rounds, Fort Hood, Killeen, Texas.

Gorey, K. M., & Leslie, D. R. (1997). The prevalence of child sexual abuse: Integrative review adjustment for potential response and measurement biases. *Child Abuse and Neglect, 21*(4), 391–398.

Groesbeck, G., Bach, D., Stapleton, P., Banton, S., Blickheuser, K., & Church, D. (2016). The Interrelated Physiological and Psychological Effects of EcoMeditation: A Pilot Study. Presented at Omega Institute, October 15, 2016.

Hart, J. (2012). *The national CV of Britain: A non-PC history of Britain.* London: Edfu.

Hidaka, B. H. (2012). Depression as a disease of modernity: Explanations for increasing prevalence. *Journal of Affective Disorders, 140*(3) 205–214.

Horton, R. (2004). *The dawn of McScience.* New York Review of Books, 51(4), 7–9.

Hui, K. K. S., Liu, J., Marina, O., Napadow, V., Haselgrove, C., Kwong, K. K.,…Makris, N. (2005). The integrated response of the human cerebro-cerebellar and limbic systems to acupuncture stimulation at ST 36 as evidenced by fMRI. *NeuroImage, 27*, 479–496.

Ingelfinger, F. (1977). Health: A matter of statistics of feeling. *New England Journal of Medicine,* February 24, 448–449.

Kanter, E. (2007). *Shock and awe hits home.* Washington, DC: Physicians for Social Responsibility.

Karatzias, T., Power, K., Brown, K., McGoldrick, T., Begum, M., Young, J.,…Adams, S. (2011). A controlled comparison of the effectiveness and efficiency of two psychological therapies for posttraumatic stress disorder: Eye Movement Desensitization and Reprocessing vs. Emotional Freedom Techniques. *Journal of Nervous and Mental Disease, 199*(6), 372–378.

Kardiner, A. (1941). *The Traumatic Neuroses of War.* New York, NY: P. B. Hoeber.

Kip, K. E., Elk, C. A., Sullivan, K. L., Kadel, R., Lengacher, C. A., Long, C. J.,…Diamond, D. M. (2012). Brief treatment of symptoms of post-traumatic stress disorder (PTSD) by use of Accelerated Resolution Therapy (ART). *Behavioral Sciences, 2*(2), 115–134. doi:10.3390/bs2020115.

Krystal, J. H., Rosenheck, R. A., Cramer, J. A., Vessicchio, J. C., Jones, K. M., Vertrees, J. E.,…Stock, C. (2011) Adjunctive risperidone treatment for antidepressant-resistant symptoms of chronic military service–related PTSD: A randomized trial. *JAMA, 306*(5), 493–502.

Lane, J. (2009). The neurochemistry of counterconditioning: Acupressure desensitization in psychotherapy. *Energy Psychology: Theory, Research, and Treatment, 1*(1), 31–44. doi:10.9769.EPJ.2009.1.1.JRL.

Lipton, B. H. (2008). *The biology of belief: Unleashing the power of consciousness, matter and miracles.* Carlsbad, CA: Hay House.

McCrory, E. J., De Brito, S. A., Sebastian, C. L., Mechelli, A., Bird, G., Kelly, P. A., & Viding, E. (2011). Heightened neural reactivity to threat in child victims of family violence. *Current Biology, 21*(23), R947-R948.

McGowan, P. O., Sasaki, A., Huang, T. C., Unterberger, A., Suderman, M., Ernst C,…Szyf, M. (2008). Promoter-wide hypermethylation of the ribosomal RNA gene promoter in the suicide brain. *PLoS One, 3*(5), e2085. doi:10.1371/journal.pone.0002085.

McNally, R. J. (2006). Cognitive abnormalities in post-traumatic stress disorder. *Trends in Cognitive Sciences, 10*(6), 271–277.

Monson, C. M., Schnurr, P. P., Resick, P. A., Friedman, M. J., Young-Xu, Y., & Stevens, S. P. (2006). Cognitive processing therapy for veterans with military-related post- traumatic stress disorder. *Journal of Consulting and Clinical Psychology, 74,* 898–907.

Nader, K. (2003). Memory traces unbound. *Trends in Neurosciences, 26*(2), 65–72.

Napadow, V., Kettner, N., Liu, J., Li, M., Kwong, K. K., Vangel, M.,…Hui, K. K. (2007). Hypothalamus and amygdala response to acupuncture stimuli in carpal tunnel syndrome. *Pain, 130*(3), 254–266.

Petrovic, P., Ekman, C. J., Klahr, J., Tigerström, L., Rydén, G., Johansson, A. G., ... & Landén, M. (2015). Significant gray matter changes in a region of the orbitofrontal cortex in healthy participants predicts emotional dysregulation. *Social Cognitive and Affective Neuroscience.* Published online June 15, 2015. doi:10.1093/scan/nsv072.

Poulter, M. O, Du, L., Weaver, I. C., Palkovits, M., Faludi, G., Merali, Z., Szyf, M., & Anisman, H. (2008). GABAA receptor promoter hypermethylation in suicide brain: Implications for the involvement of epigenetic processes. *Biological Psychiatry, 64*(8), 645–652. doi:10.1016/j.biopsych.2008.05.028.

Reich, W. (1927). *Die Funktion des Orgasmus: Zur Psychopathologie und zur Soziologie des Geschlechtslebens,* Vienna, Austria: Internationaler Psychoanalytischer Verlag.

Rodriguez, T. (2012). Can eye movements treat trauma? Scientific American, December 19, 2012. Retrieved from http://www.scientificamerican.com/article/can-eye-movements-treat-trauma.

Scaer, R. C. (2007). *The body bears the burden: Trauma, dissociation, and disease* (2nd ed.). New York, NY: Routledge.

Scaer, R. C. (2012). *The dissociation capsule.* Retrieved from http://www.traumasoma.com/excerpt1.html.

Schiller, D., Raio, C. M., & Phelps, E. A. (2012). Extinction training during the reconsolidation window prevents recovery of fear. *JoVE (Journal of Visualized Experiments),* (66), e3893-e3893.

Seal, K. H, Maguen, S., Cohen, B., Gima, K. S., Metzler, T. J., Ren, L.,...Marmar, C. R. (2010). *Journal of Traumatic Stress, 23*(1), 5–16.

Sebastian, B., & Nelms, J. (2016). Emotional Freedom Techniques (EFT) for posttraumatic stress disorder: A systematic review and meta-analysis. *Explore: The Journal of Science and Healing* (in press).

Shapiro, F. (1989). Eye movement desensitization and reprocessing: A new treatment for posttraumatic stress disorder. *Journal of Behaviour Therapy and Experimental Psychiatry, 20,* 211–217.

Smith, C. (2012, December 29). Soaring cost of military drugs could hurt budget. *American Statesman.* Retrieved from http://www.statesman.com/news/news/national-govt-politics/the-soaring-cost-of-military-drugs/nThwF.

Spielberg, J. M., McGlinchey, R. E., Milberg, W. P., & Salat, D. H. (2015). Brain network disturbance related to posttraumatic stress and traumatic brain injury in veterans. *Biological Psychiatry, 78*(3), 210–216.

Sroufe, L. A., Egeland, B., Carlson, E. A., & Collins, W. A. (2010). *The development of the person: The Minnesota Study of Risk and Adaptation from Birth to Adulthood.* New York, NY: Guilford.

Sussman, D., Pang, E. W., Jetly, R., Dunkley, B. T., & Taylor, M. J. (2016). Neuroanatomical features in soldiers with post-traumatic stress disorder. *BMC neuroscience, 17*(1), 1.

Swanson, L. (2014). *Neuroanatomical terminology: A lexicon of classical origins and historical foundations.* New York, NY: Oxford University Press.

Tal, K. (2013, February 26). PTSD: The futile search for the "quick fix." *Scientific American.* Retrieved from http://news.yahoo.com/ptsd-futile-search-quick-fix-163000525.html.

Traquair, H. M. (1944). *An introduction to clinical perimetry* (4th ed.). St. Louis, MO: C. V. Mosby.

Trickett, P. K., Noll, J. G., & Putnam, F. W. (2011). The impact of sexual abuse on female development: Lessons from a multigenerational, longitudinal research study. *Development and Psychopathology, 23*(02), 453–476.

Tronick, E., Als, H., Adamson, L., Wise, S., & Brazelton, T. B. (1979). The infant's response to entrapment between contradictory messages in face-to-face interaction. *Journal of the American Academy of Child Psychiatry, 17*(1), 1–13.

Tronick, E. Z. (1989). Emotions and emotional communication in infants. *American Psychologist, 44*(2), 112.

Tym, R., Beaumont, P., & Lioulios, T. (2009). Two persisting pathophysiological visual phenomena following psychological trauma and their elimination with rapid eye movements: A possible refinement of construct PTSD and its visual state marker. *Traumatology, 15*(3), 23–33.

Tym, R., Dyck, M. J., & McGrath, G. (2000). Does a visual perceptual disturbance characterize trauma-related anxiety syndromes? *Journal of Anxiety Disorders, 14*(4), 377–394.

U.S. Department of Health and Human Services. (2012). *Child maltreatment 2011.* Washington, DC: Administration for Children and Families, Administration on Children, Youth and Families, Children's Bureau. Retrieved from http://www.acf.hhs.gov.

Van der Kolk, B. A. (2014). *The body keeps the score: Brain, mind, and body in the healing of trauma.* New York, NY: Viking.

Van Ijzendoorn, M. H., Schuengel, C., & Bakermans-Kranenberg, M. J. (1999). Disorganized attachment in early childhood: Meta-analysis of precursors, concomitants, and sequelae. *Development and Psychopathology, 11*(2), 225–250.

Vasterling, J. J., & Brewin, C. R. (Eds.). (2005). *Neuropsychology of PTSD: Biological, cognitive, and clinical perspectives.* New York, NY: Guilford.

Wells, S., Polglase, K., Andrews, H. B., Carrington, P., & Baker, A. H. (2003). Evaluation of a meridian-based intervention, Emotional Freedom Techniques (EFT), for reducing specific phobias of small animals. *Journal of Clinical Psychology, 59*, 943–966. doi:10.1002/jclp.10189.

Whitaker, R. (2011). *Anatomy of an epidemic: Magic bullets, psychiatric drugs, and the astonishing rise of mental illness in America.* New York, NY: Random House.

White, R., & Wild, J. (2016). "Why" or "How": The Effect of Concrete Versus Abstract Processing on Intrusive Memories Following Analogue Trauma. *Behavior therapy, 47*(3), 404–415.

Winnicott, D. W. (1956). *Primary maternal preoccupation.* London: Tavistock.

Wolpe, J. (1958). *Psychotherapy by reciprocal inhibition.* Palo Alto, CA: Stanford University Press.

Index

www.ingramcontent.com/pod-product-compliance
Lightning Source LLC
Chambersburg PA
CBHW081159270326
41930CB00014B/3222